WILHELM TELL

The Library of Liberal Arts
OSKAR PIEST, FOUNDER

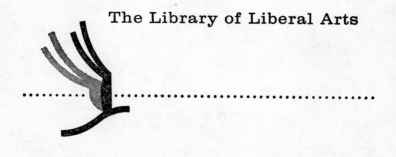

The Library of Liberal Arts

WILHELM TELL

JOHANN CHRISTOPH FRIEDRICH VON SCHILLER

A verse translation, with an Introduction, by

GILBERT J. JORDAN

Professor of German, Southern Methodist University

• •

The Library of Liberal Arts

published by

THE BOBBS-MERRILL COMPANY, INC.
A Subsidiary of Howard W. Sams & Co., Inc.
Publishers • Indianapolis • New York • Kansas City

Johann Christoph Friedrich von Schiller: 1759-1805

WILHELM TELL was first performed on March 17, 1804

. . . .

PT2473
.T3
J6

TRANSLATOR'S PREFACE

In 1959 the bicentennial of the birth of Friedrich Schiller was celebrated in many parts of the world. On this occasion scholars and students of literature surveyed the accomplishments of the great German poet and dramatist, began new research and re-evaluations, and called his works to the attention of the reading public and the theaters. It was felt all too keenly, however, that Schiller could not fully reach the English-speaking world until some wholly new translations of his works were available. This was especially true in the case of his last great drama, *Wilhelm Tell*, since its standard translation was well over a century old. The present translation was undertaken in order to remedy the situation.

The task of the translator is to render carefully and honestly, in present-day, living language, the content and the style of the original. This does not mean, as some translators think, that he must translate literally at every point; nor does it imply that he should adapt freely and produce a new version, as others maintain. The content of a classic like Schiller's *Tell* cannot ever be separated from its form and style. Of course, in some degree every good translation is inevitably a new version, but this new version must be accurate and must not sacrifice the special artistic qualities of the original or its poetic music.

In the case of the present translation it was clear that the striking, eloquent poetry of Schiller could not be translated into stilted literal verse. These lines had to be rendered in fresh and vigorous language that can speak to us today—yet speak in the poet's own form and style. Therefore the

entire verse pattern—the regular iambic pentameter of the
main body of the play and the varied meters of the lyrical
preludes and the monks' chorus—has been retained with
few exceptions. The occasional rhymes in lyrical passages,
pithy statements, and the concluding lines of especially
dramatic speeches have been preserved as exactly as possible without sacrificing the natural order and correct
choice of words.

In the course of composing this new translation, I have
benefited to some degree from consulting older English
versions. I wish to acknowledge my indebtedness to the
1847 translation of *Wilhelm Tell* by Sir Theodore Martin,
which has been considered the best for more than a hundred years but has become unacceptable for modern use.
Certain words and lines in the play seem to have only one
natural verse rendition, but comparison will show that
both the text and tone of the present translation are alto-
gether different from those of any other English version
and that the occasional identical lines are rare. A far
greater influence on choice of words and phrasing came
from the use of the glossaries and notes of two excellent
old German-language editions of the play, the first by
Robert W. Deering (Boston: D. C. Heath and Company,
1894) and the second by Arthur H. Palmer (New York:
Henry Holt and Company, 1898). These two editions,
which have become classics in the textbook field, and the
Schiller Symposium (Austin: The University of Texas,
1960), as well as various Schiller biographies and histories
of literature, were also valuable aids in the preparation of
the Introduction and the Notes.

The greatest assistance, however, came from the careful
reading, the discerning criticism, and the brilliant sugges-
tions for improvement by George Schulz-Behrend and
Megan Laird Comini, who gave much time to the revision

and encouragement to the translator. I also wish to acknowledge the assistance of my son, Terry G. Jordan, who
prepared the map and gave frequent aid in all matters per-
taining to geography. Information given in the Notes on
musical settings was furnished by Alvin D. Jett.

The completion of the work was facilitated by a grant
from the Graduate Council of the Humanities at Southern
Methodist University, assisted by the Danforth Foundation. This assistance and the personal interest of Albert C.
Outler and other members of the Council are greatly
appreciated.

G. J. J.

Dallas, Texas
August 1964

CONTENTS

WILHELM TELL

ILLUSTRATIONS

(following page xvi)

INTRODUCTION

Friedrich Schiller (1759–1805) is Germany's best-known dramatist and one of the world's great poets of freedom and idealism. Out of his early rebelliousness and his yearning for liberty, there developed the mature principles of personal and political independence that became the main concern of his energetic mind and the major theme of his writings. His life was a restless process of self-development and growth, unrelenting in its drive to portray human grandeur as he conceived it. His amazingly productive career grew out of this realm of ideas and shows hardly a note of personal experience.

It seems almost paradoxical that this intellectual and idealistic writer, whose elevated and stirring lines give practically no suggestion of his own life and generally present historical rather than contemporary situations, could ever have been the people's poet. But such is indeed the case, and it is no exaggeration to claim that Schiller became, and perhaps still remains, the most popular of all German dramatists. Although average citizens of the mid-nineteenth century probably did not completely fathom his ideals and his revolutionary spirit, they recognized in him a champion of freedom, representative government, and bourgeois morality, and they made him the spokesman for national unity and people's rights. Certainly no German poet's lines have ever been the household possession of so many people as those of Schiller. Of course, this popularity alone could not have established Schiller's claim to literary greatness; he could also hold his own in the finest theaters and command the respect of thoughtful men everywhere.

I. Schiller's Life and Works

A look at the poet's humble origin illuminates his struggles to win a place in the world and sets off his literary achievement. Schiller was born on November 10, 1759, in Marbach on the Neckar in Württemberg, Germany, the home of his mother, Elisabeth Dorothea (nee Kodweiss) Schiller (1732–1802). The house in which he was born still stands, restored and well preserved though slightly altered, and is open to the public; most of the mementos and literary documents are in the Schiller National Museum, also in Marbach. The poet's father, Johann Kaspar Schiller (1723–1796), was a man of modest education but sufficient ambition to publish two books of his own, one on economics and the other on arboriculture. He was in turn a soldier, barber and field surgeon, recruiting officer, and finally gardener in the service of Duke Karl Eugen of Württemberg. The parents instilled in the youth the firm principles and the traditional piety of their Swabian Protestant heritage.

During Schiller's early years the family moved frequently. In 1760 his mother took the two children, Friedrich and his older sister, Christophine, for a brief visit to his father's winter quarters at Würzburg during the Seven Years' War. In 1763 the family lived for a short time in Ludwigsburg, the duke's residence near Stuttgart. In 1764 they moved to Lorch. Here young Friedrich, who was a good student but not a child prodigy, received his first instruction in the village school from Pastor Moser, whose influence and example made him decide to become a preacher. The year 1766 found the family back in Ludwigsburg, where the boy attended the Latin school until 1773. These years provided occasional visits to the theater, as well as glimpses of the lavish pomp of Duke Karl

Eugen's court, a sharp contrast to the solid, religious, middle-class life of the Schiller family.

The training at the Ludwigsburg Latin school was meant to be the first stage of preparation for theological studies at the University of Tübingen; but when the duke established a new military academy at his Castle Solitude near Stuttgart, the thirteen-year-old Schiller was compelled to enroll. The youth had begun to demonstrate considerable promise as a student, and the duke wanted him for the service of Württemberg, offering a free education for the boy and continued favors for the father. This offer, which the family did not dare refuse, was certainly an honor; but it was unwelcome, for the move subjected the young man to the regimented life of a military academy and forced him to shift from theology to law. Naturally he arrived expecting to be displeased, and in the course of the years he let his displeasure grow into rebellious resentment. School discipline was extraordinarily repressive, arousing in him a hatred of authoritarianism that stayed with him through his whole life. Nevertheless, the academy provided him with many intellectual and social advantages, as well as time for private study and reading, and in spite of his resentment he conformed to its rules and even gained the duke's favor by flattery and oratorical talent. Some measure of relief came in 1777, when the academy was moved to Stuttgart and Schiller was permitted to transfer from law to medicine.

Medicine appealed to young Schiller more than law, but more rewarding still were the lectures by a young Professor Abel, who introduced philosophical and literary materials into his courses. Soon Schiller and a group of like-minded students smuggled in and read works by Shakespeare, Lessing, Goethe, and some of the "Storm and Stress" poets, such as Klinger, Leisewitz, and Schubart.

Schiller was greatly impressed when one of these idolized poets, Johann Wolfgang Goethe—later to become his close friend—visited Stuttgart and looked on while awards were presented to the students, including Schiller himself. Even earlier, during the school years at Castle Solitude, Schiller and some of his friends had tried their hand at writing, but now under the influence of the rebellious "Storm and Stress" literature their inner revolt against absolutism became more intense and they were stimulated to express their feelings in plays and stories. Besides writing some youthful poems, which he published in his *Anthologie* in 1782, Schiller began his first drama, *Die Räuber* (*The Robbers*). He completed the play during his last three years of study and published it anonymously, with borrowed funds, in 1781, one year after he graduated from the academy into the army as a poorly paid regimental surgeon.

In spite of its extravagance, *Die Räuber* is the most impressive of Schiller's early dramas. Set in the eighteenth century, the play deals with the struggle of a noble robber against tyranny and injustice. In the spirit of Schiller's youthful titanism, it challenges the very foundation of eighteenth-century civilization and the system of absolute rule. No wonder some of the ruling aristocracy took offense. An anecdote tells of a prince who said that if he had been God, and if in the act of creating the world he had foreseen that Schiller's *Robbers* would be written there, he would not have created the world at all.

The play brought Schiller considerable fame almost immediately. It was first performed in Mannheim on January 13, 1782, under the well-known director Dalberg. This performance, which Schiller attended without official leave, was received with great enthusiasm. Soon the play appeared in Hamburg, Leipzig, and Berlin, and a second edition was published in Frankfurt and Leipzig in the same year.

Then, in May, Schiller returned to Mannheim, again without leave, in order to see another performance. As it turned out, Dalberg could not grant the playwright's request for a performance at this time, and Schiller had to return to Stuttgart without seeing the play. Nevertheless, he enjoyed his brief stay and found himself well received, especially by Dalberg, who held out some hope for employment at the theater provided that Schiller could obtain a release from his service in Württemberg. Upon his return, Schiller sensed all the more sharply the great contrast between the foreign theatrical world and his own miserable lot as regimental surgeon.

While the young man was waiting for Dalberg to procure his release from his post, the duke learned of the second jaunt to Mannheim, and for this breach of military discipline he put the playwright under arrest for two weeks and denied him all travels abroad. The situation was further aggravated by a complaint from Switzerland over a satirical reference in the play. This induced the duke to reprimand Schiller and to forbid further playwriting. Fearing a life of imprisonment like that which the poet Schubart was then suffering, Schiller deserted and fled to Mannheim in September 1782, in the company of his friend Streicher. Taking assumed names, the two made an exciting escape by night during a time of high festivity at the duke's new castle.

Under the circumstances of the desertion and escape, Dalberg could not come to Schiller's rescue without involving himself in controversy, and the young man waited in vain for an appointment as theater poet. Fearful and nearly penniless, he turned to revising for publication his second play, *Die Verschwörung des Fiesco zu Genua* (*The Conspiracy of Fiesco at Genoa*), which he had written in a stage version before his flight and had hoped to see in the Mannheim theater. At this critical moment he received an invitation from the widowed mother of a Stuttgart schoolmate, Wilhelm von Wolzogen, to come to the village of Bauerbach. The destitute young man gladly took refuge there and spent about eight months in the village, at first more or less alone, and finally under the care of his patroness and her daughter. Schiller grew very fond of the girl, Charlotte, but Frau von Wolzogen, no matter how kind and motherly she was to him, did not intend to have him marry her daughter. During this time Schiller revised his *Fiesco* again for the stage, began writing a third play, which he called "Luise Millerin," and did some preliminary work on *Don Carlos*. It was 1783 before Dalberg called him to Mannheim to become theater poet, and in 1784 *Fiesco* was presented. The play deals with the fight for political independence in the city-state of Genoa, and ends tragically when Fiesco, after joining the republic's battles for freedom, conspires to gain the throne for himself and thus brings disgrace and defeat upon the cause.

During his stay in Mannheim, Schiller completed his "Luise Millerin," and, upon the suggestion of the famous actor Iffland, titled it *Kabale und Liebe* (*Love and Intrigue*). The play, which portrays the struggle of the middle classes against the ruling aristocracy, shows more vividly than its predecessors the evils of absolutism. In addition it brings to the stage more dramatically than ever before in German literature the pathos of family tragedy. Chiefly for this reason, the drama was successful on the stage and has had a more lasting appeal than any of Schiller's early plays.

A friendship developed between Schiller and Margarete Schwan, the daughter of his publisher at that time, and he corresponded with her later while he lived in Gohlis, but her father opposed whatever plans for marriage Schiller

Courtesy of the German Information Center

Portrait of Schiller by Simanowitz (1793)
In the Schiller National Museum, Marbach, Germany

The Tell Monument in Altdorf, Switzerland

They will be talking of this archer Tell
As long as mountains stand on their foundations.

(Lines 2041–2042)

Wilhelm Tell Chapel on Lake Lucerne

Inhospitable cliffs rise steeply up;
They stare at him, without a ledge to grasp.

(Lines 2160–2161)

Open Air Performance at Interlaken, Switzerland

Unless you shoot, the boy and you *both* die.

(Line 1900)

may have cherished. The new theater poet also won the love of the unhappily married Charlotte von Kalb, largely through her enthusiasm over the performance of *Kabale und Liebe*. A highly charged love affair ensued between the poet and Charlotte, who must have been a charming and brilliant woman but something of a siren. During this time Schiller also met Duke Karl August of Weimar, his later patron, and read the first act of *Don Carlos* in his presence at Darmstadt. As a consequence the duke conferred upon him the honorary title of councilor, which carried with it some status, but no stipend.

Schiller's connection with the Mannheim theater lasted only one year. In order to earn a livelihood, he turned to journalism and published the *Rheinische Thalia,* a periodical he continued to issue under the mastheads *Thalia* and *Neue Thalia* until 1793. Then Schiller's life took a fortunate turn, through his correspondence and subsequent friendship with Gottfried Körner and a circle of other admirers in and around Leipzig and Dresden, who invited the poet to join them. Under the generous patronage of Körner, Schiller lived in Gohlis, near Leipzig, from April to September of 1785. Here he wrote his well-known, extremely effusive "Ode to Joy," which Beethoven later set to music and incorporated into his *Ninth Symphony*.

Eager to be closer to his friend Körner, Schiller went to Dresden and through Körner's generosity lived almost two years, from 1785 to 1787, in a little garden house in nearby Loschwitz. The years he spent there were happy ones, and they represent a turning point in his literary career. Although he continued to spend some time on his *Thalia,* the major accomplishment of his Loschwitz years was the revision and completion of *Don Carlos*. The first three acts, written in Mannheim under the influence of Charlotte von Kalb and published in the *Rheinische Thalia,* dealt mainly with the love of Don Carlos, son of Philip II, for his stepmother, Elizabeth. In the completed play, rewritten in blank verse, the original family tragedy is expanded into a political tragedy. This led to the play's inordinate length and lack of unity. Nevertheless, it is the added material—the new Marquis von Posa plot and Posa's inspired pleas for tolerance, enlightenment, and liberty—that has given the play its universal and lasting appeal; the eloquent speech that culminates in the words "Grant us freedom of thought" still speaks as powerfully today as it did in Europe on the eve of the French Revolution. At performances of the drama given during the Hitler regime, the fiery lines called forth so much applause that the play was banned from the stage.

With the completion of *Don Carlos,* Schiller had out-grown his earlier turbulence and achieved the restraint and balance that characterize his later works. He was ready for Weimar, the literary capital of Germany, where the most famous German poets of the time—men like Wieland, Goethe, and Herder—had been brought together under the patronage of the ruling Duchess Anna Amalia and her son, Duke Karl August. Schiller first visited Weimar in 1787. There he was caught again briefly in the magic circle of Charlotte von Kalb, until, through Wilhelm von Wolzo-gen, he renewed his acquaintance with Charlotte von Lengefeld (1766–1826) and her sister Karoline, whom he had met casually in Mannheim in 1784. Now he was drawn closer to them. They corresponded during the spring of 1787, and after Schiller moved that summer to Volkstadt, near their home, they saw one another frequently. Schiller became engaged to Charlotte in 1789, and they were married in 1790.

During his stay in Volkstadt, Schiller worked on his first historical study, *The Revolt of the United Netherlands,* which he completed in 1788. His early historical writings, which grew out of his studies for *Don Carlos,* are not objective history, for which the time was not yet ripe and for which he had neither the preparation nor the inclination; instead, they are quite literary in form and content, at their best in portraying great men of history. Largely because of the success of his first book, Schiller was named professor of history at Jena in 1789. He began his professorship with misgivings but pursued his studies industriously. Between 1791 and 1793 he completed his second volume, *The History of the Thirty Years' War,* which is important chiefly because it prepared the way for his later monumental drama *Wallenstein.*

Schiller's intellectual life was further enriched by his deep interest in classical literature and philosophy. He prepared a German version of Euripides' *Iphigenia in Aulis* and wrote two excellent poems on Greek themes, "The Gods of Greece" (1788) and "The Artists" (1789). His studies of Kantian philosophy and aesthetics, to which he was directed by his friend Körner, resulted in the poems and several brilliant essays of the middle 1790's. In his essay "On Gracefulness and Dignity," which he published in his *Neue Thalia* in 1793, Schiller sets forth his conception of the cultured man. In "The Aesthetic Education of Man," published in *Die Horen* in 1795, he develops his theories on the role of beauty in the education of mankind. In the third of his great essays, "On Naïve and Sentimental Poetry" (1795), which grew out of his correspondence and discourses with Goethe, he expounds his differentiation between the natural and intuitive, or "naïve," literature of the ancients and the subjective, philosophical, and imaginative, or "sentimental," literature of his own time.

Schiller had met Goethe at the von Lengefelds in 1788,

but the two men were not immediately drawn together. Goethe reacted unfavorably to Schiller's works, which still savored too much of "Storm and Stress" to suit his taste, while Schiller envied the more fortunate poet and felt a strong antipathy toward his work, as reflected in his critical review of Goethe's *Egmont*. Then, too, Goethe was ten years older than Schiller and had enjoyed greater financial security, better educational opportunities, and broader experience. Although he had been persuaded to use his influence to secure for Schiller the professorship at Jena, five years passed before a close friendship matured.

Meanwhile, in 1791 Schiller had a severe bout with a respiratory illness that plagued him from time to time for the rest of his life, and he went to Karlsbad for his convalescence. When reports of his illness reached a circle of admirers in Denmark, they conferred on him a generous three-year stipend. During these years the Schillers paid visits to Körner and other friends in Leipzig and to the Schiller family in Ludwigsburg, thus re-establishing close family relations after a separation of ten years.

During the Jena years, Schiller won the friendship of the philologist Wilhelm von Humboldt, who later was a minister of state in Prussia and the founder of the University of Berlin. Von Humboldt shared Schiller's philosophical interests and encouraged him in his study of Greek literature. Together the two men set out to mold a new German literary language and poetry in the classical style. They were joined in this project by Goethe. Schiller's views had become more acceptable to Goethe, as was revealed in a long conversation between the two men after a lecture in Jena,[1] and in 1794 Schiller invited Goethe to assist him in publishing a new journal, *Die Horen* (*The*

---

[1] See Karl Berger, *Schiller. Sein Leben und seine Werke* (Munich, 1923), II, 257 ff.

Hours, 1795–1797). Thus started what turned out to be one of the most rewarding literary friendships in history. Through extensive correspondence and conversation they exchanged ideas, criticized each other's work, and encouraged each other to devote more time to writing. For Goethe this meant renewed interest in his *Faust* and *Wilhelm Meister* and the writing of *Hermann und Dorothea.* He wrote to Schiller: "You have provided me with a second youth and made me a poet again." [2] For Schiller it was the most vital decade of his life, characterized by a great surge of creativity that brought forth his best poems and ballads and his final series of five great historical dramas. In addition to encouraging each other, the two men also collaborated in writing the *Xenien,* literary satires in distichs, which were published in Schiller's collection titled *Almanac of the Muses.*

Although Schiller's poems lack the intensity of personal emotion usually associated with great lyric verse, the poet compensates for this missing subjective element by imbuing his poems with a profound and spirited idealism. Some of his best reflective verse was written in 1795, notably "The Promenade" and "Ideals and Life," considered by some critics to be his finest poems. The year 1797 brought forth his greatest ballads, such as "The Diver," "The Glove," and "The Cranes of Ibycus." In contrast to Goethe's short, lyrical ballads, Schiller's ballads are chiefly dramatic stories in verse form. Other 1797 poems, such as "Words of Faith" and "Hope," are among his most popular. In 1799 two poems appeared that also deserve mention: "Nänie" (Latin: *Nenia,* "Dirge"), set to music by Brahms, and "The Song of the Bell." In the latter, one of his longest and best-known poems, Schiller interweaves an

---

[2] Translated from *ibid.,* p. 276.

account of the casting of the bell with a poetic depiction of the joys and sorrows of honest middle-class people.

In 1799 Schiller moved permanently to Weimar in order to be closer to Goethe and the Weimar literary circle and to the theater. His major literary activity during these years was the writing of the trilogy *Wallenstein*. The original plans for the play date back to 1791, and it is mentioned again in 1794, but the actual writing did not begin before 1796. *Wallensteins Lager* (*Wallenstein's Camp*), which is better described as a prelude than as a full play of the trilogy, was composed for the most part in 1798 and presented on the Weimar stage. The second and third parts, *Die Piccolomini* and *Wallensteins Tod* (*Wallenstein's Death*) were completed in 1799, and the great historical tragedy was performed in its entirety and well received in Weimar the same year. *Wallenstein* is the first large-scale historical drama in German literature, moving with grand pageantry over the complex events of the Thirty Years' War; but it is above all a tragedy of character, and its greatness derives primarily from the skill with which Schiller depicts the dramatic tension within the tragic hero himself along with the external conflict between the warring powers. The drama was published in 1800 by Cotta, who became the publisher of all of Schiller's works.

With *Wallenstein*, Schiller's muse had turned once and for all to the drama, the realm which was most compatible with his gifts and in which he achieved his greatest fame. The year 1800 saw the completion and successful performance of *Maria Stuart*, another tragedy on a historical theme, but a play of an entirely different kind. There is no Shakespearean panoramic plot leading through a maze of events to the catastrophe. As in the Greek analytical plays, the central character is faced with impending catastrophe from the beginning, and the poet concerns himself primarily with the closing in of her individual fate and her triumph over death. Although Schiller was a Protestant, it was only natural that he, the poet of individual liberty, should sympathize with the imprisoned Catholic queen. As in his other historical dramas, he feels no compunction about altering known facts of history; he is always more dramatist than historian. In the case of *Maria Stuart*, he could not resist the temptation to bring Mary and Elizabeth together in a climactic scene, in which the two queens do battle with all the weapons of rhetoric and invective at the poet's command. The drama remains one of Schiller's most stageworthy plays.

His next play, *Die Jungfrau von Orleans* (*The Maid of Orleans*, 1801), which treats the story of Joan of Arc, is subtitled a romantic tragedy; but Schiller was not a poet of romanticism, and the play is only superficially romantic in such matters as the medieval setting, Joan's mystical visions, and the idealization of the virgin warrior. Intrinsically it is a tragedy of character. The play was enthusiastically received, and Schiller was given an ovation when he attended the performance in Leipzig as Körner's guest.

Meanwhile Schiller suffered serious attacks of his old lung ailment. Much recognition had come to him: he received the patent of nobility from the emperor in 1802, Prince Eugen of Württemberg befriended him, Madame de Staël of France visited him, and the King of Sweden presented him with gifts. But Schiller paid little attention, and continued to work in spite of illness and fame. In 1802 and 1803 he wrote *Die Braut von Messina* (*The Bride of Messina*), a tragedy in the Hellenistic style with choruses and a plot dramatizing the role of fate. In spite of the poet's attempts to create a play in the sublime classical manner, the characters do not achieve the statuesque grandeur of the Greek heroes and heroines. Moreover, a tragedy of fate on a "Storm and Stress" theme of fratricide was no longer acceptable to the modern theater, as Schiller himself soon realized.

As a result of his interest in the drama of other countries, and upon the urging of Duke Karl August, Schiller also translated and adapted for the stage a group of English, French, and Italian plays. Among these are Shakespeare's *Macbeth* (1801), Gozzi's *Turandot* (1802), Picard's *Parasite* and *The Nephew as Uncle* (1803), and Racine's *Phèdre* (1804). These versions were prepared for the Weimar stage, where Goethe was theater manager.

The last great drama that Schiller completed during these final, intensely productive years was *Wilhelm Tell*. The subject of the legendary Swiss hero and the Swiss fight for freedom had been discovered by Goethe, who planned to write an epic poem on the theme, but he decided to give the material to his friend Schiller for dramatic treatment. While the latter was still busy with his *Jungfrau von Orleans* in 1801, he was falsely rumored to be writing a Tell play, but it was 1803 before he actually started.

The epic scope of his subject matter caused Schiller much difficulty at first, but once the poet had brought his materials under control he wrote the play rapidly. He finished it early in 1804 and published it in October as a "new year's gift for 1805," but the first edition of seven thousand copies was soon exhausted, and a second printing of three thousand copies followed before the new year arrived. The first performances were given, to great applause, in Weimar on March 17, 1804, and in Berlin, beginning on July 4, 1804. In these early productions and in subsequent performances, especially in the middle of the century, *Wilhelm Tell* proved to be Schiller's most successful play.

Several of Schiller's plays had been acclaimed in Berlin, and in 1804, not long after the enthusiastic reception of *Wilhelm Tell,* the poet was honored in this city by presentations of his *Wallenstein, Die Jungfrau von Orleans,* and *Die Braut von Messina.* Schiller attended this play festival, and efforts were made to persuade him to take up residence in Berlin, but he chose to return to Weimar. Here he set to work again on another drama, this time on a Russian theme, but the play, *Demetrius,* remained a fragment. The great dramatist died on May 9, 1805, at the age of forty-five years and six months. Only about a year earlier he had written the monks' dirge in *Wilhelm Tell:*

> Death comes to us before our time
> And grants no respite from his power;
> He cuts us down in life's full prime
> And drags us off at any hour.
> Prepared or not to go away,
> We have to face our judgment day.
>
> (Lines 2834–2839)

Schiller's place in German literature was by no means uncontested at the time of his death. Some of the romanticists, especially the Schlegel brothers and Tieck, attacked him vigorously because they disapproved of his declamatory rhetoric and did not find enough sensuous perception and personal experience in his works. Then, too, after the Napoleonic wars and during the restoration period, the reactionary rulers feared Schiller as a dangerous revolutionary, and some theaters were closed to his works. On the whole, however, the poet had received much acclaim. He had won the friendship and esteem of Germany's greatest poet, Goethe, and of other luminaries in and out of Weimar, men like Wieland, Herder, and Jean Paul; and he had captured the interest of some of the great com-

posers, including Beethoven. Of special significance was
the growing concern of scholars and writers. His works
were translated into all important European and some Asi-
atic languages; books were published on the subject of his
flight from Württemberg and on his correspondence with
Goethe; a play about his school years, Laube's *Pupils of
the Karl Academy,* appeared in 1847; and Thomas Carlyle
wrote an appreciative biography. During the first half of
the nineteenth century, Schiller gained his great popularity among the middle-class people as a poet of freedom
and national unity. This enthusiasm reached its peak during and after the Revolution of 1848, especially in 1859,
when the one-hundredth anniversary of Schiller's birth was
celebrated.

Schiller's literary influence did not match his literary
achievement. His *Räuber* and *Die Braut von Messina* gave
impetus to a brief, unfortunate fashion for romantic fate
tragedies, frequently grotesque in their exaggeration, by
such playwrights as Werner, Müller, and Grillparzer; his
Wallenstein became the prototype for later trilogies by
Grillparzer, Hebbel, and Richard Wagner. Perhaps his
most beneficial influence was in the field of large-scale
historical drama. Here Schiller was the master craftsman,
able to transform historical and traditional subject matter
into plays of great scope and power in the heroic tradition.
His followers were not only the "epigones," or late classi-
cists, poets like Grillparzer, Platen, and Immermann, but
also realists such as Grabbe and Hebbel. The influence of
his freedom plays, especially *Wilhelm Tell,* can be seen in
Immermann's *Tragedy in the Tirol,* a play based on An-
dreas Hofer's long fight for freedom. Finally, in the realm
of versification, Schiller, along with Lessing and Goethe,
introduced and perfected iambic pentameter in German
drama. Schiller was especially adept in this verse form. He

employed it in all his great dramas beginning with his *Don Carlos* in 1787, and thus he helped to establish it in German literature as the generally accepted form for serious drama.

Schiller's popularity has declined, of course, with the rise of the modern theater. Critics of a more realistic school miss in his works a complex insight into human personality and take exception to his persistent idealism and his intention to inspire. It is true that his characters, with the exception of Wallenstein and Mary Stuart, are one-sided—either good or bad, heroes or villains. Moreover, Schiller tends to let his characters, even women and children, think and speak in masculine Schillerean style, and their motives often seem cerebral rather than emotional. What he portrays, then, are not complicated flesh-and-blood characters, such as are found in life. Rather they are figures that remind one of Greek statues, massive and monolithic in conception and shaped in clear contours— perfectly suited, in short, to a drama of ideas. His language, admittedly formal and rhetorical even in scenes of pathos, is vigorous and eloquent like the orchestration of a Beethoven symphony, and the iambic pentameter of his great dramas moves with a bold and sweeping momentum. Viewed within the heroic tradition, Schiller remains a towering figure in the literary history of Europe.

II. THEME AND HISTORICAL BACKGROUND OF *Wilhelm Tell*

Many of Schiller's writings deal in one way or another with the theme of freedom; almost all his dramas portray man's struggle against despotism at home or oppression from abroad, taking their energy from the poet's passionate desire for liberty. Schiller had had his own encounters with excessive authoritarianism, and inwardly he was resentful. Moreover, he had studied about rebellions and uprisings recorded in history—the revolt of the Netherlands against Spain, which he treated in his historical work on this subject and in *Don Carlos,* and the French liberation from the British, which is the background for his *Jungfrau von Orleans.* He had also seen the struggle acted out in his own time, as the growth of ideals of liberty during the eighteenth century culminated abroad in the American war for independence and the French Revolution. But closest of all was the threat of Napoleon, who was expanding his conquests in Europe. Napoleon had already made Switzerland a vassal state of France, and was crowned emperor in the same year in which Schiller completed his drama of Swiss freedom, *Wilhelm Tell.*

In all his early plays Schiller was concerned primarily with the pressures of despotism and with revolt against tyranny and hopeless fights for independence. By showing the evils of oppression, these plays stir the audience to an intense yearning for liberty, although the cause is always lost. In two of Schiller's later plays, *Die Jungfrau von Orleans* and *Wilhelm Tell,* political liberation is attained, but only in the latter did his subject allow a satisfying resolution of his lifelong political ideals. This play is the culmination of his treatment of the theme of freedom. It portrays not only the winning of political independence, but also a victory for human rights with the establishment of a united "nation of true brothers" (line 1449), where men can "live in liberty" (line 3290) in a free land.

The specific issue in *Wilhelm Tell* is the struggle in the Middle Ages of three Swiss cantons (Uri, Schwyz, and Unterwalden) for independence from their powerful neighbors, the Hapsburg rulers of Austria. It was not a fight for absolute political liberty; instead, the cantons desired semi-independence and home rule under the protection of the Holy Roman emperor. The Empire was a loose confederation of various provinces, duchies, principalities, and kingdoms, whose emperor was elected by and from the electors of the more powerful provinces. The cantons had been subjects of the Empire since the partition of Charlemagne's empire in 843, and in the course of centuries they had won or been granted a degree of independence. Moreover, they looked to the emperors for protection from the interference of local overlords, particularly the ambitious Hapsburgs.

By conquest and marriage, the Hapsburgs had expanded their holdings from small possessions in Switzerland to encompass most of German Switzerland and Austria, where they became the ruling dukes. Like most of the German provinces, including the three Swiss cantons, their domains were subject to the Empire. Their efforts to expand their power brought them into conflict with the Swiss. As long as the emperors were chosen from some other ruling house, the cantons could continue to be secure under the protection of the emperor; but when, in 1273, Rudolf of Hapsburg was chosen king and emperor, the Swiss cantons were faced with the predicament of having as their emperor a member of the very house against which they had sought imperial protection.

The Swiss cantons based their claim of direct allegiance to the emperor on certain charters, granted originally by Emperor Frederick II in 1231 and 1240, in return for control of St. Gotthard's road and aid in his Italian campaigns (referred to in line 912). Rudolf, the first Hapsburg emperor, did not press his private claims and even renewed the Uri charter. His successor, Adolf of Nassau, reissued both the Uri and Schwyz charters, but Albrecht of Hapsburg, chosen emperor in 1298, did not renew any of the charters. This refusal brought up the major political problem of the play. Under the charters, the Swiss cantons gave direct allegiance to the emperor and in return received his protection. Swearing allegiance to Albrecht not as emperor but as Hapsburg duke of Austria would have made the Swiss people Hapsburg vassals. The Swiss revolt, then, was an uprising not against the Empire, but against Austria. By winning this contest, which actually extended far beyond the scope of Schiller's drama, the cantons maintained their status of direct dependence on the Empire.

Albrecht of Hapsburg is the tyrannical sovereign of Schiller's play. Although he was stern and ambitious, he was not so merciless as tradition and the drama have depicted him. He did not install cruel governors like Schiller's Gessler and Landenberg, and there was no Swiss rebellion during his reign. Nevertheless, tradition associated him with the Swiss-Hapsburg conflict, and Schiller found it dramatically effective to compress the Swiss struggle for freedom into the last three weeks of Albrecht's reign, which Schiller moved back from the spring of 1308 to the fall of 1307. Albrecht was murdered by his nephew, Duke John of Swabia, the Parricida of the play, on May 1, 1308 (see lines 2939–3015 for Schiller's account), and he was succeeded by Heinrich, Duke of Luxembourg, who renewed the charters in 1309. In the subsequent contest for the crown between Ludwig of Bavaria and Frederick of Austria, the Swiss sided with Ludwig and defeated the attacking Austrians in the battle of Morgarten pass in 1315. This is the great battle prophesied by Attinghausen (lines 2439–2447).

The historical events of the play concern not only the successful revolt of the cantons, but also the forming of a union, which symbolizes the establishment of a united nation (see the Rütli meeting, Act II, scene 2). Actually the present constitution of the Swiss confederation, which makes Switzerland an independent nation, was not adopted until 1814, but there were several previous agreements. As early as 1246–1247, three of the cantons (Unterwalden, Schwyz, and Lucerne) formed a league for common defense against Hapsburg control. During the interregnum (1256–1273) the Swiss cantons had no emperor to whom they could give allegiance and who might protect them. To hold their own against the Hapsburg threat, in 1260 Uri, Schwyz, and Unterwalden formed a protective league, which was renewed in 1291 and 1315. These agreements were the basis for the Rütli oath of confederation and self-defense in the play. They were later extended to other cantons as these joined the league one by one, until the present confederation resulted.

Various legends and traditions grew up around the long Swiss struggle for freedom, finding their way into old chronicles, history books, and several Tell plays antedating Schiller's drama. The sources Schiller used were primarily the sixteenth-century *Swiss Chronicle* by Tschudi and a *History of the Swiss Confederation* by Johannes Müller. Although he knew that the characters and stories were a medley of fact and fiction, he included them in the play and adapted them to his dramatic purpose. The chief issue of the play, namely, the fight for freedom, and some of the characters—kings and emperors—are historical, but factual history makes no mention of most of the characters in the play, including Wilhelm Tell himself. They belong to the colorful pageantry of folklore and legend. Many names used by Schiller appear in the sources, where the persons play roles or appear in some capacity related to those in the play. Among them are Gessler, Attinghausen, Gertrud, Reding, Fürst, Melchtal, Baumgarten, and Tell and his family. Some names (such as Konrad Hunn and Hans auf der Mauer) appear in Swiss documents and were simply taken over into the play as names for fictional characters; other names were selected because they are typically Swiss (for example, Kuoni, Werni, Ruodi, Rösselmann, and Petermann). Finally, there are some roles (notably Berta and Rudenz), some episodes, and one complete scene (Act III, scene 2) that Schiller invented himself. Even Rudolf der Harras, Gessler's master of the horse, is fictional in the role he plays; and the appearance of the Brothers of Mercy is anachronistic, inasmuch as this order was not organized until long after the time of the play.

Schiller condensed and unified his source materials to illustrate his great themes. He constructed three interlocking plots showing various aspects of the struggle against tyranny—first, the people, oppressed by fear and high-handed acts of the governors, gradually uniting and moving toward action; secondly, Tell, the freedom-loving individualist, who is harassed by the cruel governor until he is driven to act, and by his independent act maintains his personal freedom and becomes a popular hero; finally, the native Swiss nobles, who are suspicious of outside influence (Attinghausen) or become disillusioned with privilege and its abuse (Rudenz and Berta). All three move toward a common purpose by different routes, until at the end of the play their interests coincide and they are united.

Parricida is excluded from this union because his act was selfish and willful, tending toward anarchy. In the Parricida scene Schiller made one further attempt to justify Tell's slaying of the tyrant Gessler by contrasting it to Parricida's assassination of the emperor for personal gain. Perhaps this scene, if it is necessary at all, would be more effective if the condemnation of Parricida's act were not made by Tell himself, but the confrontation of these two men is dramatic and gives Tell an opportunity to show his compassion.

The Wilhelm Tell plot is excellent folklore, and the great playwright used it with spectacular dramatic effect. The story of the simple, honest, peace-loving hunter, with its famous apple-shooting scene, the storm and rescue, and the murder of the tyrannical governor, accounts for much of the popular appeal and the success of the play. But it is the people's fight for freedom that dominates and gives unity to the action. The people collectively are the real heroes of the drama, and the audience, sensing the universality of their efforts, identifies itself with their struggle. In this sense, then, the play remains meaningful to us today when human liberty is still threatened, as it was in the past, and when we all "must work to win it every day" (line 1491), as Tell wins his own life and liberty.

GILBERT J. JORDAN

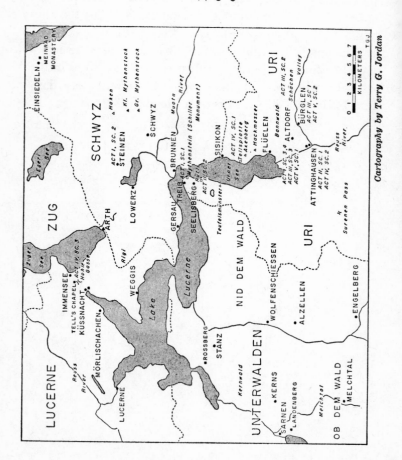

THE WILHELM TELL COUNTRY

Lake Lucerne and the Four Forested Cantons, showing the location of each act and scene of the play

Cartography by Terry G. Jordan

WILHELM TELL

CHARACTERS

HERMANN GESSLER, imperial governor or viceroy in
    SCHWYZ and URI

WERNER, BARON VON ATTINGHAUSEN, banneret and free
    noble

ULRICH VON RUDENZ, his nephew

Countrymen of SCHWYZ

WERNER STAUFFACHER

KONRAD HUNN

ITEL REDING

HANS AUF DER MAUER

JÖRG IM HOFE

ULRICH DER SCHMIED

JOST VON WEILER

Countrymen of URI

WALTER FÜRST

WILHELM TELL

RÖSSELMANN, the priest

PETERMANN, the sacristan

KUONI, the herdsman

WERNI, the hunter

RUODI, the fisherman

Countrymen of UNTERWALDEN

ARNOLD VOM MELCHTAL
KONRAD BAUMGARTEN
MEIER VON SARNEN
STRUTH VON WINKELRIED
KLAUS VON DER FLÜE
BURKHARD AM BÜHEL
ARNOLD VON SEWA

PFEIFER VON LUCERNE
KUNZ VON GERSAU
JENNI, fisherman's (RUODI's) son
SEPPI, herdsman's (KUONI's) boy servant

GERTRUD, STAUFFACHER's wife
HEDWIG, TELL's wife, FÜRST's daughter
BERTA VON BRUNECK, a rich heiress

Countrywomen

ARMGARD
MECHTHILD
ELSBET
HILDEGARD

TELL's *sons*

WALTER
WILHELM

Soldiers

FRIESSHARD
LEUTHOLD

RUDOLF DER HARRAS, GESSLER'S Master of the Horse

JOHANNES PARRICIDA, Duke of Swabia

STÜSSI, the ranger

HORNBLOWER, the Ox of Uri

A ROYAL COURIER

OVERSEER

HEAD MASON, JOURNEYMEN, LABORERS

PUBLIC CRIERS

BROTHERS OF MERCY (monks of the Order of Charity)

TROOPERS of GESSLER and LANDENBERG

MANY COUNTRYMEN and WOMEN from the Forest Cantons

ACT ONE

Scene I

A steep and rocky shore of Lake Lucerne,[1] opposite Schwyz.

(The lake forms an inlet into the land. Not far from the shore is a hut. The FISHERMAN'S SON *is rowing about in his boat. Across the lake are seen the green meadows, the villages, and the farmhouses of Schwyz in bright sunlight. To the spectator's left are the peaks of the Haken, covered with clouds; to the right, in the distant background, ice-capped mountains are visible. Before the curtain rises, the Kuhreihen,* Alpine cowherd's melody,[2] *and the harmonious sound of cowbells are heard. These sounds continue for some time after the curtain rises.)*

FISHERMAN'S SON *(singing in the boat)*

Alpine Cowherd's Melody

The waters are smiling, inviting the land;
The boy lies asleep upon the green strand;
    He hears a sweet music
    Like flutes in the skies,

---

[1] In German *Vierwaldstättersee,* or "Lake of the Four Forest Cantons." The four cantons bordering on the lake are Lucerne (*Luzern*), Schwyz, Uri, and Unterwalden. Only the last three are involved in the fight for freedom treated in the play.

[2] The *Kuhreihen,* literally "cow dance," is a sort of folk tune without words that can be played on the alpenhorn. It is used again to herald the celebration at the end of the play.

5   Like voices of angels
             In paradise.
     And when he awakens in blissful joy,
     The waters are playing, caressing the boy.
             He hears in the distance
10   A call from the sea:
             You are mine, dear sleeper,
             I'll draw you to me.

     HERDSMAN (*on the mountain*)

     Variation of the Alpine Cowherd's Melody

             Farewell, sunny meadows;
             Farewell, you green grasses!
15   The herdsman must leave you;
             The summer soon passes.
     We'll come back to these mountains, return every spring,
     When the cuckoo calls, when the world wakes to sing,
     When the flowers are clothing the earth anew,
20   When the brooks are flowing, and fields are in dew.
             Farewell, sunny meadows;
             Farewell, you green grasses!
             The herdsman must leave you;
             The summer soon passes.

     ALPINE HUNTER (*appearing on the opposite side on
             the top of the cliff*)

     Second Variation

25   The mountains are rumbling and shaking the trail;
     The hunter fears nothing, his footing won't fail;
             He strides along boldly
             On fields of sheer snow;
             No springtime is dawning;

No grasses will grow. 30
And under his feet a nebulous sea,
Where cities and men he no longer can see.
But a break in the clouds
Gives a glimpse of a scene:
Far down by the water, 35
The meadows of green.[3]

(*The landscape changes, and a muffled roaring is heard
from the mountains. Shadows of clouds pass over the scene.*)

(RUODI, *the fisherman, comes out of the hut.* WERNI, *the
hunter, climbs down from the cliff.* KUONI, *the herdsman,
comes with a milk pail on his shoulder.* SEPPI, *his boy
servant, follows him.*)

RUODI

Hurry, Jenni! Pull in the boat and come!
I see the fog and hear the glacier rumbling;
The Mythenstein [4] is putting on its shroud,
And from the weatherhole [5] the wind is blowing. 40
I think the storm will come before we know it.

---

[3] The three parts of the lyrical prelude were set to music by Franz
Liszt in three songs titled "The Fisherman's Son," "The Herdsman,"
and "The Alpine Hunter" (Opus 292, 1845 and 1855). Each of the
parts has been given at least one other musical setting: the first by
Edward MacDowell, "The Fisher Boy" (Opus 27, No. 3, 1890); the
second by Robert Schumann, "The Herdsman's Farewell" (Opus 79,
No. 22); and the third by Franz Schubert (Opus 37, No. 2, 1817).

[4] A steep but not very high rock on the shore of Lake Lucerne,
near the locale of the scene. Schiller evidently meant one of the
Mythenstock peaks.

[5] A literal translation of *Wetterloch,* a term applied to gorges,
caves, or crevices in the mountains from which the wind blows before a storm.

KUONI

It's going to rain all right; my sheep are grazing
More eagerly, and Watcher paws the ground.

WERNI

The fish are leaping, and the water hen
45 Is diving down. A storm is on the way.

KUONI (*to the boy*)

See, Seppi, that our cattle are not straying.

SEPPI

I hear brown Lisel's bell not far from here.

KUONI

Then none is gone, because she goes the farthest.

RUODI

Melodious bells you have there, master herdsman.

WERNI

50 And splendid cattle, too. Are they your own?

KUONI

I'm not so rich. They are my gracious Lord
Von Attinghausen's, and only in my charge.

RUODI

Just see that cow; she wears her collar proudly.

KUONI

She knows quite well that she must lead the herd;
If I should take it off, she would not graze. 55

RUODI

That makes no sense! A stupid animal—

WERNI

Hold on! The animals have reason, too.
We hunters learn that when we're hunting chamois.
When they go out to graze, they wisely post
A sentinel to prick his ears and warn, 60
With piercing call, whenever hunters come.

RUODI (*to the* HERDSMAN)

You're driving home your herd?

KUONI

The pasture's bare.

WERNI

Good luck then, friend!

KUONI

I wish the same for you!
Some hunters don't return from trips like yours.

RUODI

Look, who's the man that's running in such haste? 65

WERNI

I know him well; it's Baumgart from Alzellen.

(KONRAD BAUMGARTEN *dashes in, breathless.*)

BAUMGARTEN

For God's sake, boatman, take me in your boat!

RUODI

Here now, what is the hurry?

BAUMGARTEN

Untie the boat!
Save me from death! Take me across the lake!

KUONI

70 What is the matter, friend?

WERNI

Who's after you?

BAUMGARTEN (*to the* FISHERMAN)

Hurry, hurry, they're close upon my heels!
The viceroy's horsemen, they are after me!
If they should catch me, it would mean my death.

RUODI

But tell me, why are the troopers after you?

BAUMGARTEN

75 Just save me first, and then I'll answer questions.

WERNI

You're stained with blood. What in the world has
    happened?

BAUMGARTEN

The emperor's bailiff at the Rossberg castle—

KUONI

That's Wolfenschiessen! Is he after you?

BAUMGARTEN

He cannot harm me now, for I have killed him.

ALL (*shrinking back*)

May God be merciful! What have you done?   80

BAUMGARTEN

What any free man in my place would do.
Defended fairly, as it was my right,
The honor of my home and of my wife.

KUONI

You mean the bailiff has assailed your honor?

BAUMGARTEN

He would have carried out his evil purpose   85
If God and my good ax had not forestalled it.

WERNI

You struck the man and killed him with your ax?

KUONI

Oh, let us hear it all; you still have time
Before he can untie the boat from shore.

BAUMGARTEN

90 I had been felling trees in nearby woods,
When suddenly my frightened wife came running
And said the bailiff was at home and had
Commanded her to draw the bath for him,
And that he then expressed insulting wishes.
95 But she escaped to seek me out and tell me.
I then ran quickly home, just as I was,
And with my ax I blessed him in his bath.

WERNI

And you did right; no man can blame you for it.

KUONI

That tyrant! Now he has his just reward,
100 So long deserved from Unterwalden's people!

BAUMGARTEN

My deed was talked about, and now I am
Pursued—God! while we talk, I'm losing time!

(*It begins to thunder.*)

KUONI

Be quick now, boatman, ferry him across!

RUODI

It can't be done. A heavy storm is coming.
You'll have to wait.

BAUMGARTEN

                   Oh, holy God! You must.   105
I cannot wait. The least delay means death.

KUONI (*to the* FISHERMAN)

Trust God and try! We have to help a neighbor.
The same might happen any time to us.

   (*Roaring and thunder*)

RUODI

The storm is here. Look how the lake is rising!
I cannot row against the wind and waves.   110

BAUMGARTEN (*throwing his arms around* RUODI'S
        knees)

May God reward you, as you pity me.

WERNI

His life's at stake. Be merciful to him!

KUONI

He is a family man with wife and children!

   (*Repeated claps of thunder*)

RUODI

What do you mean? I also have a life
115   To lose, a wife and child at home like his.
      Just see the waters break and surge and whirl
      And boil up from the bottom of the lake.
      I'd gladly try to save the good man's life,
      But you can see it is impossible.

BAUMGARTEN (*still on his knees*)

120   Then I must fall into the tyrant's hands,
      With safety on the other shore in sight.
      Yes, there it lies. My eyes behold it clearly;
      My pleading voice can even reach the haven.
      There is the boat to ferry me across,
125   And I must stay here, helpless and despairing.

KUONI

Who's coming over there?

WERNI

                              It's Tell from Bürglen.

(TELL *enters with his crossbow.*)

TELL

Who is this man that's asking you for help?

KUONI

He's from Alzellen, and to save his honor
He had to kill the tyrant Wolfenschiessen,
130   The royal bailiff from the Rossberg castle.
      The viceroy's men are close upon his heels.

He begs the boatman to be ferried over,
But this man fears the storm and will not go.

RUODI

Look, here is Tell! He is a boatman too,
And he can say if I should risk the passage.   135

TELL

When there's a need, then all things must be risked.

(*Violent claps of thunder, as the lake surges up*)

RUODI

I am to leap into the jaws of hell?
No man in his right mind would try it now.

TELL

The true man thinks about his neighbor first.
Rely on God, and rescue this poor man.   140

RUODI

It's easy to advise when safe in harbor.
Well, here's the boat and there's the lake! You try it!

TELL

The lake may help, but not the governor.
Try it, boatman.

HERDSMEN *and* HUNTER

                    Save him! Save him! Save him!

RUODI

145 If he were my own brother or my child,
It could not be. This is St. Simon's Day,
And Jude's; [6] the sea will have its sacrifice.

TELL

We can accomplish nothing here by talking.
The hour is pressing and the man needs help.
150 Speak, boatman, are you going?

RUODI

No, not I.

TELL

Well then, for God's sake, give the boat to me.
I will attempt it with what strength I have.

KUONI

How brave!

WERNI

Just like the hunter that he is!

BAUMGARTEN

My rescuer and guardian angel, Tell!

TELL

155 Well may I rescue you from tyrant's power;
A mightier arm must save you from the storm.

---

the scene. The year is 1307.
  [6] St. Simon's and St. Jude's Day is October 28 and sets the date of

But rather fall into the hand of God
Than in the hands of men.

> (*To the* HERDSMAN)

                  Console my wife
If human fate should find me on this passage.
I've done what I could never leave undone.   160

> (*He jumps into the boat.*)

KUONI (*to the* FISHERMAN)

You are a master oarsman, yet you would not
Attempt to do what Tell has undertaken?

RUODI

And better men than I can't equal Tell;
No other man is like him in these mountains.

WERNI (*who has climbed on the cliff*)

He's shoving off. God help you, gallant boatman!   165
See how his boat is tossing on the waves!

KUONI (*on the shore*)

The waves have swallowed it. It's out of sight.
But wait, I see it now! With all his might
The brave man fights his way against the breakers.

SEPPI

Here come the viceroy's troopers at a gallop.   170

KUONI

God knows you're right. That help came just in time.

(*A band of Landenberg's troopers appears.*)

FIRST TROOPER

Give up the murderer that you are hiding!

SECOND TROOPER

He came this way. It does no good to hide him.

KUONI *and* RUODI

Whom do you mean?

FIRST TROOPER (*discovering the boat*)

Oh, damn it all, I see him!

WERNI (*above*)

175   You want that fellow in the boat? Ride on.
Ride fast, and you may overtake him still.

SECOND TROOPER

Confound it! Gone.

FIRST TROOPER (*to the* HERDSMAN *and* FISHERMAN)

You helped him get away.
You'll pay for this. Go kill their herds and flocks!
Destroy their cabins—burn them to the ground!

(*They dash off.*)

SEPPI (*following them*)

180   My little lambs!

Kuoni (*following him*)

> They're killing all my cattle!

Werni

Those murderers!

Ruodi (*wringing his hands*)

> This cries to heaven for justice!

When will a savior come to help our land?

> (*He follows them.*)

Scene II

Steinen in Schwyz.

(*A linden tree in front of* Stauffacher's *house on the highway, near a bridge.*)

> (Werner Stauffacher *and* Pfeifer von Lucerne *enter, engaged in conversation.*)

Pfeifer

Yes, yes, Herr Werner, it is as I said,
Don't swear allegiance to the Austrians;
Hold firmly to the Empire, as before.   185
May God protect you in your ancient freedom.

> (*He presses* Stauffacher's *hand cordially and is about to leave.*)

STAUFFACHER

Do stay until my wife returns. You are
My guest in Schwyz, as in Lucerne I'm yours.

PFEIFER

No, thanks. I'm on my way to Gersau now.
190 Whatever hardships you may have to bear
From greed and insolence of governors,
Endure in patience. Things can quickly change;
Another emperor might rule the realm.
Once joined to Austria, you're bound for good.

(*He leaves. Sorrowfully,* STAUFFACHER *sits down on a bench under the linden tree.* GERTRUD, *his wife, finds him like this, stands beside him, and looks at him for a while without speaking.*)

GERTRUD

195 So solemn, Werner? I no longer know you.
For days I have observed in silence how
This gloomy melancholy makes you frown.
You bear a silent sorrow in your heart.
Confide in me. I am your faithful wife,
200 And I demand that I may share your sorrow.

(STAUFFACHER *gives her his hand in silence.*)

What is it that can grieve your heart? Tell me.
Your diligence is blessed: your fortune grows;
The barns are full; your well-fed herds of cattle
And teams of horses, thoroughbred and sleek,
205 Have all been driven home from mountain pastures
To spend the winter in the spacious stables.
There stands your house, as fine as any castle,

Now newly built of costly seasoned timber
And put together by the rule and square;
From many windows gleams a homelike splendor; 210
It's gaily painted with our coat of arms
And words of wisdom, that the wanderer
May read and contemplate their deeper meaning.

STAUFFACHER

The house is fashioned and constructed well,
But oh, the ground on which it's built is shaking. 215

GERTRUD

My Werner, tell me what you mean by this.

STAUFFACHER

Not long ago I sat beneath this linden
With pleasant thoughts of our completed work,
When all at once the governor rode up.
He came from Küssnacht castle with his troopers 220
And halted in surprise before this house.
But I stood up respectfully and walked,
As it is due and proper, toward the lord
Who represents the king's judicial power
Within our lands. "Whose house it this?" he asked 225
With evil purpose, for he knew it well.
But, thinking very quickly, I replied,
"This house, sir, is the emperor's, my lord
As well as yours, and is a fief." He said,
"I am the regent in the emperor's name, 230
And do not want you farmers to build houses
Upon your own decision, and suppose
That you can live as free as lords yourselves.
I plan to put a stop to all this freedom."

235 And then he rode away defiantly
And left me standing there with troubled mind,
Reflecting on the words that he had spoken.

GERTRUD

My own dear lord and husband, will you hear
A candid word from me, your trusting wife?
240 I'm proud that I am noble Iberg's daughter;
He was a man of much experience.
We sisters sat the long nights spinning wool
When leaders of the people came to father,
And met and read together ancient charters
245 From former rulers, and then with thoughtful words
Discussed our country's welfare and condition.
I listened to those wise deliberations,
What prudent men advise and good men wish,
And quietly I kept them in my heart.
250 So listen to me now and weigh my words.
I've known for many days what's troubling you.
The viceroy holds a grudge, would like to harm you
Because he thinks you are the one to blame
That men from Canton Schwyz will not submit
255 To Austrian rule; instead they stand and cling
In loyalty and firmness to the Empire,
Just as our fathers always did before us.
Is this not true? You tell me if I'm wrong.

STAUFFACHER

It's true, all right; that's Gessler's grudge against me.

GERTRUD

260 He envies you because he sees you live
A free man on your own inheritance,
For he has none. You hold your house in fief

Directly from the Empire and may show it
As well as royal princes show their lands.
You recognize no overlord above you   265
Except the highest one in Christendom.[7]
He is a younger son of his own house,
Possessing nothing but his cloak of knighthood,
And therefore looks on every good man's fortune
With envious eyes and a malicious mind.   270
He plotted for your downfall long ago.
You stand here still unharmed, but will you wait
Till he takes out his evil spite on you?
The wise man takes precautions.

    STAUFFACHER

                          What can I do?

    GERTRUD (*moving closer to him*)

Will you take my advice? You know how, here   275
In Canton Schwyz, all honest men complain
About the viceroy's greed and cruelty.
I do not doubt that people over there
In Unterwalden and in Canton Uri
Are also weary of the hard oppression;   280
For just as Gessler plays the tyrant here,
So Landenberger rules across the lake.
No fishing boat comes over to our shores
That doesn't bring us word of some fresh evil,
Some new injustice by the governors.   285
It would be well, I think, if some of you
Good citizens would quietly take counsel
How we can best escape from this oppression.
I feel convinced that God would not forsake you

---

[7] The emperor of the Holy Roman Empire of the German nation.

290   And would be gracious to a righteous cause.
Have you no one in Uri, no close friend
To whom you may disclose your heart completely?

STAUFFACHER

Indeed I know some loyal men in Uri
And influential men of high repute
295   Whom I can trust in any secret matter.

(He stands up.)

Oh, what a storm of dangerous thoughts you waken
Within my quiet mind and heart! You shed
The light of day upon my inmost thoughts;
And what I silently forbade myself
300   To think, you speak right out with daring tongue.
Have you considered well what you advise?
You'll call a wild discord and sound of weapons
Into this peaceful valley of our land.
How can we helpless country people dare
305   To start a war against a mighty nation?
They're only waiting for a pretext now
To loose their raging hordes of men upon us,
To overrun and take our little land
And rule it as the spoils of victory,
310   And under semblance of just punishment
Destroy the ancient charters of our freedom.[8]

GERTRUD

You too are men, and you can use the ax;
And God will always help courageous men.[9]

---

[8] See the Introduction, pp. xxviii–xxxi.
[9] This dialogue in couplets is an adaptation of the Greek single-line speeches called *stichomythia*. See lines 415–422 and 433–438.

STAUFFACHER

Oh, Gertrud, warfare is a raging horror;
It will destroy our herds and kill our herdsmen.   315

GERTRUD

We must endure whatever heaven sends us,
But noble hearts will never bear injustice.

STAUFFACHER

This house that we have built delights you now.
But war, this monstrous war, will burn it down.

GERTRUD

If ever I felt chained to earthly goods,   320
I'd throw the firebrands in with my own hands.

STAUFFACHER

Your faith is in humanity, but war
Will not spare even babies in the cradle.

GERTRUD

Yet innocence still has a friend in heaven.
Look only forward, Werner, not behind.   325

STAUFFACHER

We men can bravely fight, and fighting die;
But you must know what women's fate will be.

GERTRUD

The final choice lies open to the weakest;
A leap into the water makes me free.

STAUFFACHER (*embracing her*)

330 Who presses such a heart against his breast
Can fight with pleasure for his hearth and home
And never fear the royal army's might.
I'm going to Uri now, just as I am;
A trusted friend lives there. He's Walter Fürst,
335 And his opinions are the same as mine.
I'll also find the noble banneret
Lord Attinghausen. Though of higher rank,
He loves the people and respects our customs.
I will take counsel now with these two men
340 To plan defense against our enemies.
Good-by, and while I am away from home,
Conduct the business of our household wisely.
Give generous gifts and hospitality
To pilgrims going to the house of God
345 And to the monks collecting for the cloister.
Stauffacher's house is not concealed. It stands
Right out beside the road, a welcoming roof
For all the wanderers who come our way.

(*As they move backstage,* WILHELM TELL *and* BAUM-
GARTEN *enter at the front.*)

TELL (*to* BAUMGARTEN)

And now you have no further need of me.
350 Go to this house and enter. It's the home
Of Stauffacher, a friend of the oppressed.
But there he is himself—come, follow me!

(*They walk toward him; the scene changes.*)

Scene III

A public square at Altdorf.[10]

(On a hill in the background a fortress is seen under construction, so far advanced that the shape of the whole can be made out. The back is finished, but the front is still being constructed. The scaffolding on which workmen are climbing up and down is still in place. The slater is perched on the highest point of the roof. Everybody is in motion and at work.)

Overseer *(driving the workmen with his staff)* [11]

Don't stop so long! Come on! Let's have the stones!
Be quick! And now bring up the lime and mortar!
When the viceroy comes, he's got to see   355
Results. You're slower than a pack of snails.

(To two laborers carrying loads)

Is that a load? Go carry twice as much!
Such lazy idlers, always slacking off!

First Workman

This is too much, that we must carry stones
To build the dungeon to imprison us.   360

Overseer

What are you grumbling there? A sorry gang

---

[10] The chief town in Canton Uri. This canton is the setting of all but two of the fifteen scenes of the play.

[11] Schiller calls the overseer a *Fronvogt,* that is to say, a man who oversees the *Frondienst,* the compulsory labor performed, instead of payment of taxes, by vassals for the feudal lord.

That's fit for nothing but to milk the cows
Or loaf about and wander in the hills.

OLD MAN (*stopping to rest*)

I can't go on.

OVERSEER (*shaking him*)

Get up, old man, and work!

FIRST WORKMAN

365   Have you no heart at all, that you drive on
To heavy work a man who's barely able
To drag himself along?

HEAD MASON *and* WORKMEN

It is outrageous!

OVERSEER

Go mind your business. Here, I am in charge.

SECOND WORKMAN

Say, overseer, what will they call this fortress
370   That we're building?

OVERSEER

The Uri fortress. And you
Will bend your stubborn necks beneath this yoke.

WORKMEN

The Uri fortress!

OVERSEER

What's so funny now?

SECOND WORKMAN

You plan to keep down Uri with this hut?

FIRST WORKMAN

Let's see how many molehills of this kind
You'd have to pile up till a mountain grows   375
That's equal to the smallest one in Uri.

(*The* OVERSEER *walks to the back.*)

HEAD MASON

I'll throw my hammer in the deepest lake
Because I used it on this cursed place.

(TELL *and* STAUFFACHER *enter.*)

STAUFFACHER

I wish I'd never lived to see such things.

TELL

It isn't good to stop here. Let's go on.   380

STAUFFACHER

Am I in Uri, in the land of freedom?

HEAD MASON

Oh, sir, if you could see the dungeons deep
Below the towers! Whoever's kept down there
Will never hear the cock crow in the morning.

STAUFFACHER

385 Oh God! [12]

HEAD MASON

Just see the bastions, see the buttresses,
So strongly built they'll stand eternally.

TELL

What hands built up, hands can tear down again.

(*He points at the mountains.*)

This house of freedom God himself created.

(*A drum is heard, and people enter, carrying a hat on a
pole. A* PUBLIC CRIER *follows them. Women and children
press tumultuously after.*)

FIRST WORKMAN

390 Why do they beat the drum? Look there!

HEAD MASON

What circus
Parade is this, and why the pole and hat?

CRIER

In the emperor's name! Give heed!

WORKMEN

Be still and listen!

---

[12] One of several short lines in the original.

CRIER

Look at this hat, you men of Uri, look!
It will be raised upon a towering pole
In Altdorf, at the highest spot in town.   395
And this is what the governor decrees:
Give honor to the hat as though to him;
By kneeling down and taking off your hats
Show that you honor it. By this the king
Will see just how obedient you are.   400
If any one of you defies this order,
His life and goods are forfeit to the king.

(*The people laugh out loud, the drum is heard, and
they pass by.*)

FIRST WORKMAN

What new outrageous scheme has he thought up
This time? We should give honor to a hat!
Has anybody heard of such a thing?   405

HEAD MASON

We are to bend our knees before a hat!
What kind of joke is this to play on people?

FIRST WORKMAN

Now if it were the royal crown—but no,
It is the Austrian hat; I saw it hang
Above the throne, where fiefs are handed out.   410

HEAD MASON

The hat of Austria! It is a trick
That will betray us to the Austrians.

WORKMEN

No honest man submits to such an outrage.

HEAD MASON

Come, let us talk it over with the others.

(*They go to the back of the stage.*)

TELL (*to* STAUFFACHER)

415 You see now how things are. Good-by, friend Werner.

STAUFFACHER

Where are you going, Tell? Don't hurry off.

TELL

My family needs me now. I'll say good-by.

STAUFFACHER

My heart is full of things to say to you.

TELL

A heavy heart will not grow light from words.

STAUFFACHER

420 And yet our words could lead us on to action.

TELL

Our only course is patience now, and silence.

STAUFFACHER

Shall we then bear what is unbearable?

TELL

Hotheaded rulers never last for long.
When sudden storms arise within these gorges,
We put our fires out, the boats all come   425
To harbor, and the mighty spirit moves
Across the land without a trace of harm.
Let everyone stay quietly at home,
For peace is granted to the peaceful man.

STAUFFACHER

You think so?

TELL

          A snake strikes only when provoked.   430
They will at last grow weary by themselves
When they see all the country staying calm.

STAUFFACHER

We could do much if we would stand together.

TELL

In shipwreck each does best to save himself.

STAUFFACHER

Can you so coldly leave the common cause?   435

TELL

It's safest to rely upon oneself.

STAUFFACHER

United will the weak grow mighty too.

TELL

The strong man will be strongest when alone.

STAUFFACHER

Your fatherland, then, cannot count on you
440   When in despair it turns to self-defense?

TELL (*giving him his hand*)

Tell saves a missing lamb from the abyss,
And yet you think he will forsake his friends?
Don't call me into your debates or ask
Me for my views; I cannot weigh and compare.
445   But if you need me for a special task,
Then call on Tell. He will not fail you there.

(*They leave on different sides. A sudden tumult
starts around the scaffolding.*)

HEAD MASON (*rushing over*)

What happened?

FIRST WORKMAN (*coming forward, calling*)

The slater slipped and tumbled from the roof.

(BERTA *enters with her attendants and runs up.*)

BERTA

Has he been badly hurt? Hurry! Save him!
450   If I can help you rescue him, here's gold!

(*She throws her jewelry among the people.*)

HEAD MASON

Your gold! You nobles think all can be bought
For gold! When you have torn away a father
From his children, a husband from his wife,
When you have brought down misery on the world,
You think you can repay with gold! Get out!   455
We all were happy men before you came.
With you, despair has come into our land.

BERTA (*to the* OVERSEER, *who is returning*)

Is he alive?

(*The* OVERSEER *shakes his head.*)

Unlucky fortress built
With curses, curses will inhabit you!

(*Exeunt.*)

SCENE IV

WALTER FÜRST's *dwelling.*

(WALTER FÜRST *and* ARNOLD VOM MELCHTAL *enter at the same time from opposite sides.*)

MELCHTAL

Herr Walter Fürst—

WALTER FÜRST

You must remain in hiding.   460
We are beset by spies. What if you're seen?

MELCHTAL

Is there no news from Unterwalden yet?
No news from Father?—I cannot endure
To lie here idly like a prisoner.
465   What have I done that is so criminal
That I must hide out like a murderer?
I broke that rascal's finger with my staff
When he, upon the governor's command,
Attempted to unhitch my yoke of oxen
470   And right before my eyes to drive them off.

WALTER FÜRST

You are too rash. He was the viceroy's man,
And he was sent upon your lord's command.
You had been judged at fault and had to yield
To their decision, hard as it might be.

MELCHTAL

475   Was I to stand and listen while that brute
Brazenly taunted me, and said a farmer
Who wanted bread could pull the plow himself?
It cut me to the heart when he unyoked
And took the splendid oxen from the plow.
480   They butted with their horns and bellowed low,
As if they had a feeling of injustice.
Then I was overcome with righteous anger,
And losing self-control, I struck the servant.

WALTER FÜRST

If we old men can scarcely hold our peace,
485   How can these younger men control themselves?

MELCHTAL

All my concern is for my father now.
He needs my care, and I am far away.
I know the viceroy holds a grudge against him
Because he always fought for right and freedom.
For this they will abuse the poor old man,   490
With no one there to shield him from mistreatment.
Whatever happens, I must go to him.

WALTER FÜRST

Just wait and try to bide your time in patience
Until some news is brought to us from Kernwald— [13]
Get back! I hear a knocking at the door.   495
Perhaps the viceroy's messenger has come.
You are not safe from Landenberger's power,
For tyrants give assistance to each other.

MELCHTAL

They're teaching us what we should do.

WALTER FÜRST

                                        Go in.
I'll call you back when it is safe again.   500

(MELCHTAL *goes in.*)

Poor boy, I do not dare confess to him
What dark suspicions trouble me. Who's knocking?

---

[13] In German the word is *Walde* ("forest"), but obviously Kernwald (Forest of Kerns) is meant. Melchtal lives near Kerns at the edge of the Kernwald.

Each time I hear a knock, I fear the worst.
Deceit, suspicion lurk on every side.
505 The messengers of violence intrude
Upon the privacy of homes. It seems
That we must fit our doors with locks and bolts.

    (*He opens the door and starts back surprised when*
      WERNER STAUFFACHER *enters.*)

Whom do I see? You, Werner! Well, by heaven!
A dear and honored guest. No better man
510 Has ever stepped across this threshold yet.
You have a hearty welcome in this house!
What brings you here? What do you seek in Uri?

    STAUFFACHER (*extending his hand to him*)

The good old times and good old Switzerland.

    WALTER FÜRST

That's what you bring with you. It does me good;
515 The very sight of you can warm my heart.
Sit down, my friend, and tell me how you are,
And how you left your wife, your gracious Gertrud,
Whom all know well as Iberg's prudent daughter.
All wanderers from German lands who go
520 To Italy by Meinrad's monastery
Sing praises of your hospitable house.
But tell me, did you come here straight from Flüelen,
Or did you take a look at other places
Before you set your foot upon this threshold?

    STAUFFACHER (*sitting down*)

525 I did indeed behold a new construction,
Displeasing and astonishing to me.

WALTER FÜRST

Yes, you have seen things clearly at one glance.

STAUFFACHER

It's never been like this in Canton Uri.
We've never heard of any fortresses;
The only stronghold here has been the grave.   530

WALTER FÜRST

It is a grave of freedom. You have named it.

STAUFFACHER

Herr Fürst, I tell you frankly why I came.
It was not idle curiosity.
No, worry weighs upon me now. I left
Behind oppression, and I find it here.   535
What we have suffered is intolerable,
And there's no end to all this tyranny.
For centuries we Swiss have prized our freedom,
And we are used to being treated well.
Such things were never known in all this land,   540
As long as herdsmen drove their herds to pasture.

WALTER FÜRST

What they are doing is without example.
Our noble Lord von Attinghausen, too,
Who saw and still recalls the good old days,
Has said himself that we cannot endure it.   545

STAUFFACHER

In Unterwalden serious things have happened,
And are repaid in blood. Herr Wolfenschiessen,

The royal bailiff at the Rossberg castle,
Expressed desires for forbidden fruit;
550   And when he tried to wrong most shamefully
The wife of Baumgart who lives in Alzellen,
The husband killed the fellow with an ax.

WALTER FÜRST

The judgments of the Lord are always just.
Baumgarten, did you say? A moderate man.
555   I trust he has been saved and hidden well.

STAUFFACHER

Your son-in-law delivered him from danger.
I'm keeping him in hiding now in Steinen.
And he has told me something still more dreadful
That happened lately near the town of Sarnen.
560   It makes the heart of any good man bleed.

WALTER FÜRST (*attentive*)

Go on and tell me.

STAUFFACHER

                    Well, there lives in Melchtal,
Just where you enter, coming up from Kerns,
An honest man named Heinrich von der Halden,[14]
Whose voice has weight in his community.

WALTER FÜRST

565   We know him well. But tell me what has happened.

---

14 Melchtal's father.

STAUFFACHER

When Landenberger, for some small offense,
Inflicted punishment upon the son
And ordered that his oxen be unyoked,
The son knocked down the servant and escaped.

WALTER FÜRST (*in great excitement*)

But tell me now—what happened to the father?   570

STAUFFACHER

Then Landenberger summoned him and said
That he must bring the son to him at once.
And when the old man truthfully declared
That he knew nothing of the fugitive,
The viceroy had his torturers come in—   575

WALTER FÜRST (*springing forward and trying to take
    him to the other side*)

Be quiet!

STAUFFACHER (*with rising voice*)

        "Though your son escaped, I still
Have you!" he said, and had the man held down;
And then they pierced his eyes with sharpened spikes.

WALTER FÜRST

Merciful heaven!

MELCHTAL (*running in*)

            They pierced his eyes, you say?

STAUFFACHER (*astonished, to* WALTER FÜRST)

580 Who is this man?

MELCHTAL (*seizing him with convulsive violence*)

They pierced his eyes? Speak up!

WALTER FÜRST

Oh, pitiable man.

STAUFFACHER

Who is he then?

(WALTER FÜRST *signals to him.*)

It is the son? Almighty God!

MELCHTAL

And I
Cannot be with him now. And both his eyes?

WALTER FÜRST

Control yourself! Endure it like a man.

MELCHTAL

585 It's all on my account. The guilt is mine.
He's blind? He's really blind—completely blinded?

STAUFFACHER

It's true. The springs of sight have all run dry.
He'll never see again the sunlight's splendor.

WALTER FÜRST

Oh, spare his heartache!

MELCHTAL

Never see again!

(*He presses his hand to his eyes and is silent for a few moments; then he turns from one to the other and speaks in a gentle voice, choking with tears.*)

Our eyesight truly is a precious gift   590
From heaven above. All creatures on the earth,
All happy living beings, seek the light;
Even the plants turn gladly toward the sun.
But he must sit and grope in endless darkness,
Eternal light, and never be refreshed   595
By dark green meadows and by gorgeous flowers,
Nor ever see the glaciers' reddish glow.
To die is nothing—but live, and never *see!*
That's misery. Why do you look at me
So pityingly? I have two seeing eyes   600
And cannot give them to my blinded father—
No single ray of all this sea of light
That floods into my eyes with blinding brilliance.

STAUFFACHER

And now I must increase your grief still more,
Instead of healing it. He's even more   605
In need, for they took everything he had.
The viceroy left him nothing but his staff,
To wander blindly now from door to door.

MELCHTAL

The poor old man has nothing but his staff.
610 They stole it all, and took his eyesight too,
This common prize of even the poorest man.
Don't talk to me of waiting now, or hiding.
Oh, what a wretched coward I have been
That I just thought of *my* security
615 And not of yours! I let you stay behind,
A hostage in the hands of cruel tyrants.
All cowardly precaution, leave me now!
I'll think of nothing but of bloody vengeance.
I will go home. No one can hold me back!
620 I'll find the governor among his troopers
And will demand my father's eyes from him.
My life and safety do not matter now,
If I can cool my burning, monstrous pain
And ease it in the lifeblood of this tyrant.

(*He starts to leave.*)

WALTER FÜRST

625 Stay here! What can you do? He lives in Sarnen,
Where he's secure within his lordly castle
And only laughs at all our helpless rage.

MELCHTAL

And if he lived up yonder on the ice
Of Schreckhorn peak, or higher, where the Jungfrau
630 Is veiled eternally in mist,[15] I'd make

---

[15] The Schreckhorn and the Jungfrau are two of the highest peaks in the Bernese Oberland. In Schiller's day these peaks were considered inaccessible.

My way to him. With twenty of my friends
Who think as I, I'll crack his fortress open.
And if no one will follow me, if you,
Concerned about your houses and your herds,
Will bend your necks beneath the tyrant's yoke,   635
I'll call together herdsmen in the mountains,
And there, beneath the canopy of heaven,
Where men think clearly and their hearts are sound,
I'll tell them of this great atrocity.

STAUFFACHER (*to* WALTER FÜRST)

It's gone too far. Do we intend to wait   640
Until the worst—

MELCHTAL

            What worst is there to come
That we should fear, when eyes no longer see—
No longer are secure within their sockets?
Are we defenseless then? Why did we learn
To draw the crossbow, swing the battle-ax?   645
Why, every creature's furnished with a weapon
That he may use in fear and desperation.
The baited stag will show his dreaded antlers
And hold at bay a pack of barking hounds;
The chamois hurls the hunter down the chasm;   650
The docile and domesticated ox,
That friend of man, who bends his burdened neck
So patiently beneath the yoke, will leap
When he is angered, whet his mighty horns,
And throw his enemy up toward the clouds.   655

WALTER FÜRST

If all three cantons thought as we three do,
We might be able to accomplish something.

STAUFFACHER

If Uri calls, if Unterwalden helps,
We men of Schwyz will stand by our alliance.

MELCHTAL

660 In Unterwalden I have many friends.
     Each one would gladly risk both life and limb
     If others stand by him and give support.
     You are the trusted fathers of our country,
     And next to you I'm no more than a boy.
665 Therefore I must in modesty refrain
     From speaking at our council of the cantons.
     But don't reject my judgment and advice
     Because I'm young and inexperienced.
     I'm not impelled by hot, impetuous blood,
670 But by the power of a painful grief
     So great that it might move the stones to pity.
     You too are heads of families, and fathers,
     And you must wish to have a virtuous son
     Who wants to honor and respect his father,
675 To take good care of him and guard his eyes.
     Oh, just because you have not suffered harm
     In person or in property, because
     Your eyes move in their sockets bright and sound,
     You must not stand aloof from our distress.
680 The tyrant's sword hangs over you as well.
     You turned the land against the Austrians;
     My father's crime was nothing more than that.
     You share his guilt; you'll have his punishment.

STAUFFACHER (*to* WALTER FÜRST)

If you'll decide, then I'm prepared to follow.

WALTER FÜRST

First let us hear the noblemen's advice,   685
The lords of Sillinen and Attinghausen.
Their influential names will win us friends.

MELCHTAL

Where is a name in all these mountain ranges
More highly held than your name—or than yours?
The people put their trust in names like these;   690
They stand for honest worth in all the land.
You have a rich inheritance of virtue,
And you've increased this store abundantly.
Why hear the nobles? Let us alone take action.
I think we must rely upon ourselves,   695
For then we can control our own defense.

STAUFFACHER

The nobles are not pressed so hard as we.
The torrent that is raging in the valleys
Has not engulfed the highlands even now.
But they will not withhold their help from us   700
Once they have seen the country take up arms.

WALTER FÜRST

Were there a judge between us and our foe,
Then right and law would govern the decision.
But our oppressor also is our emperor
And highest court. Our God must help us now   705
Through our own strength. You search out men in Schwyz,
And I will go and rally friends in Uri.
But whom are we to send to Unterwalden?

MELCHTAL

Send me. No one is more concerned than I.

WALTER FÜRST

710 I cannot let you leave. You are my guest,
And I must answer for your safety now.

MELCHTAL

No, let me go. I know the secret paths
And I have friends enough who'll give me shelter
And gladly hide me from our enemies.

STAUFFACHER

715 Oh, let him go. There are no traitors there,
For tyranny is so despised and dreaded
That no man will become a tyrant's tool.
And in the lower part of Unterwalden
Baumgart can win adherents for our cause.

MELCHTAL

720 But how can we communicate in safety
And not arouse suspicions in the tyrants?

STAUFFACHER

It would be best to meet at Treib or Brunnen,
Where many trading ships go in and out.

WALTER FÜRST

We cannot do our work so openly.
725 Hear my suggestion. By the western shore,
On our left hand when going down to Brunnen,

Close to the Mythenstein, a meadow lies
Right in the woods; the herdsmen call it Rütli
Because the forest was uprooted here.[16]

(*To* MELCHTAL)

The borders of our cantons meet up there,   730

(*To* STAUFFACHER)

And in a short and easy passage, too,
A boat can carry you from Canton Schwyz.
We can go there by lonely mountain trails,
And quietly deliberate at night.
Let each of us bring ten well-trusted men   735
Who are at one with us and with our plans.
This way we can discuss the common cause
And with God's help decide what's to be done.

STAUFFACHER

That's what we'll do. Now let me have your hand,
And Melchtal, give me yours; and as we three   740
Now join our hands, united in assurance
That we will stand together honestly,
So may our cantons stand together too,
Through life and death for our defense of freedom.

WALTER FÜRST *and* MELCHTAL

Through life and death!

(*They hold their hands clasped together in silence
for some moments.*)

---

[16] The name comes from the verb *roden,* meaning "to uproot" or
"clear the trees"; hence, a clearing or meadow.

MELCHTAL

745   Father, my blinded father!
You cannot see the day of freedom dawn,
But you shall hear it. When from peak to peak
The signal fires send out their flaming message,
And tyrants' castles fall into our hands,
750 The Swiss will come as pilgrims from these lands
And bring to you the news of freedom won.
Then in your night shall dawn the rising sun.[17]

(*They part.*)

---

[17] When Goethe read the first act, he said, "That really is not a first act, but a whole play, and truly first rate" (Karl Berger, *Schiller. Sein Leben und seine Werke* [Munich, 1923], II, 667).

ACT TWO

Scene I

The castle of BARON VON ATTINGHAUSEN.[1]

(*A Gothic hall, decorated with coats of arms and helmets. The* BARON, *an old man of eighty-five, tall and noble in stature, leans on a staff tipped with chamois horn, and is dressed in a fur coat.* KUONI *and six other vassals are standing around him with rakes and scythes.* ULRICH VON RUDENZ *enters in a knight's costume.*)

RUDENZ

I'm here, Uncle. Tell me what you want.

ATTINGHAUSEN

First let me by our ancient custom share
The morning cup with my good servants here.   755

      (*He drinks from a cup which is then passed around.*)

Time was when I could be in field and wood,
Directing them at work with my own eyes,
Just as my banner led them into battle;
But now I only play the overseer,
And if the warming sun won't come to me,   760
I can no longer seek it on the mountains.

---

[1] The ruins of the castle may still be seen near Attinghausen on the Reuss River, south of Altdorf in Uri. The date of this episode seems to be November 8, 1307, ten days after Act I.

And thus, in small and ever smaller circles,
I'm slowly moving toward the last and smallest,
Where all of life will cease. I'm nothing more
765 Than my own shadow now; soon just a name.

KUONI (*going to* RUDENZ *with the cup*)

I pledge you, sir!

(RUDENZ *hesitates to accept the cup.*)

Don't hesitate to drink.
One cup, one heart—that is the saying here.

ATTINGHAUSEN

Go, children, and tonight when work is done,
We'll talk about political affairs.

(*The vassals leave.*)

ATTINGHAUSEN (*to* RUDENZ)

770 I see you armed and dressed as for a journey;
You're on your way to Altdorf to the castle?

RUDENZ

Yes, Uncle, and I cannot linger now.

ATTINGHAUSEN (*sitting down*)

In such a hurry? Is your time of youth
So meagerly prescribed and measured out
775 That you can't spare a moment for your uncle?

RUDENZ

I see my presence is not needed here.
I have become a stranger in this house.

ATTINGHAUSEN (*after having looked at him intently
      for some time*)

Indeed you are a stranger here. Your home
Is now a foreign place. Oh, Uli, Uli!
I hardly know you. You strut about in silk,   780
And wear a peacock feather for display,
And throw a purple cloak around your shoulders;
You look disdainfully upon the peasant
And turn aside, ashamed at cordial greetings.

RUDENZ

I'll gladly show him the respect that's due him,   785
But I deny the rights that he demands.

ATTINGHAUSEN

Our country suffers from the king's displeasure,[2]
And all good men are troubled in their hearts
At such tyrannical abuse of power
As we must suffer. You alone remain   790
Unmoved by all our common grief and pain.
You turn away, disloyal to your people,
And stand among our country's enemies,
Scorning our cares and seeking idle pleasures,
Courting the princes' favors, while here at home   795
Your fatherland lies badly scourged and bleeding.

RUDENZ

The land is much oppressed. But why, my uncle?
Who is it that has plunged it into trouble?

---

[2] Albrecht, who is called king, as well as emperor or kaiser, is displeased because the Swiss cantons have resisted his private (Hapsburg) claims. See lines 804–806.

You only need to speak an easy word
800 To be released at once from all oppression
And gain a gracious emperor as well.
But woe to those who shut the people's eyes
And lead them to oppose the country's welfare.
These men, for their own gain, prevent the cantons
805 From swearing any Austrian allegiance,
As all around the other lands have done.
It flatters them to sit among the nobles.
They want to call the emperor their lord
In order not to have a lord at all.

ATTINGHAUSEN

810 Must I hear such a thing—and from your lips?

RUDENZ

You urged me on to speak; then let me finish.
What role is it that you yourself are playing?
Have you no higher pride than to live here
As banneret or village magistrate
815 And be the ruler of these lowly herdsmen?
Would it not be more laudable a choice
To render homage to our royal lord,
Ally yourself with all his brilliant court,
Than stay at home, the peer of your own vassals,
820 And play the magistrate among the peasants?

ATTINGHAUSEN

Oh, Uli, Uli! I can see it all;
The tempter's voice has reached your willing ears
And sent a vicious poison to your heart.

RUDENZ

Yes, I will not pretend. My very soul
Is deeply hurt by strangers' taunts and scoffing,   825
When they refer to us as peasant nobles.
I cannot bear to see all noble youths
Win honors under Hapsburg's royal banners,
While I must stay here on our property
In idleness, day in, day out, and waste   830
The springtime of my life in common chores.
In other places glorious deeds are done;
A world of fame stirs just beyond these mountains.
My helmet and my shield hang rusting here.
The thrilling sound of martial drums and trumpets,   835
The herald's call, inviting to the lists,
Will never press into these mountain valleys
Where I can only hear the herdsman's songs,
And cowbells ringing in monotony.

ATTINGHAUSEN

Poor blinded boy, seduced by empty splendor—   840
Renounce your native land, and be ashamed
Of good and ancient customs of your fathers!
The day will come when you, with bitter tears,
Will yearn for home and for your native mountains.
And then the herdsman's simple melody,   845
Which fills you now with boredom and contempt,
Will overwhelm your heart with painful longing
When you are hearing it in distant places.
Oh, mighty is the love of fatherland!
The foreign, evil world is not for you,   850
For at the proud imperial court you'll be
A stranger to yourself and to your heart.

The world demands a different sort of virtue
From that which you've acquired within these valleys.
855 But go then if you must, and sell your soul;
Take land in fief and be a prince's vassal
When you could be a ruler and a prince
Upon your own inheritance and soil.
Oh, Uli, Uli! Stay among your people
860 And do not go to Altdorf. Don't forsake
The sacred causes of your fatherland.
I am the last one of my line. My name
Will end with me. There hang my shield and helmet;
They will be put beside me in the grave.[3]
865 And must I think, when breathing out my life,
That you are only waiting for my death
To go in haste before the feudal court,
And as a fief receive from Austria
The noble lands that I received from God?

RUDENZ

870 It's useless to resist the kaiser's will.
The world belongs to him. Will we alone
Be stubborn and persist in our attempt
To break the mighty chain of his possessions
That he has powerfully drawn around us?
875 The courts of law are his. So are the markets.
The highways too are his, and every pack horse
That crosses the St. Gotthard pass is taxed.
We are entangled as within a net,
Encircled by his spreading lands and power.
880 And will the Empire shield us? Can it even
Defend itself against the Austrians?

---

[3] The burial of shield and helmet with the last of a line was an old custom.

If God will not, no emperor can help us.
How can we trust in any emperor's word
If he, when pressed for money or the needs
Of war, may pawn or even sell the towns   885
That went for refuge to his royal eagle? [4]
No, Uncle, it is wisdom and precaution,
In days of great dissension and disorder,
To be allied with such a mighty leader.
The emperor's crown will pass from house to house—   890
It has no memory of faithful service.
But gaining favor of hereditary
Lords is sowing seed for future harvest.

ATTINGHAUSEN

Are you so wise? And do you claim to see
More clearly than your noble sires, who fought   895
With life and fortune for the gem of freedom?
Sail to Lucerne and ask the people there
How Austrian rulers weigh the cantons down!
Soon they will come and count our sheep and cattle,
And measure off and tax our mountain pastures.   900
They'll take the hunting rights for all the game
In our own woods, and place the tollgate barrier
Across our bridges and beside our gates,
Impoverish us to purchase more possessions
And fight their battles with our life and blood.   905
If we must shed our blood, then let it be
For our own cause. Then we will buy our freedom
Far cheaper than their bondage.

---

[4] The questions are real enough. The emperor did not always have
as much power as some of the dukes and ruling princes within the
Empire, and he might give the cities over to some powerful vassal in
exchange for troops or money.

Wilhelm Tell

RUDENZ

What can we do,
A tribe of herdsmen, against the hosts of Albrecht?

ATTINGHAUSEN

910 First learn to know this tribe of herdsmen, boy.
I know my people well. I led them on
In battles, and I saw them take Faenza.
Just let the Austrians try to force on us
A yoke we are determined not to bear!
915 Oh, learn to see what is your heritage.
Don't throw away the pearl of your own value
In vain exchange for worthless show and glitter.
To be the leader of a freeborn people,
Who give you their devotion out of love,
920 Whose loyalty will stand through life and death—
Take pride in that. Boast that nobility.
Tie fast the native bonds and cling to them.
Hold firm and true to your dear fatherland
And cherish it with all your heart and soul.
925 The sturdy roots of all your strength are here.
Out in the foreign world you'll stand alone,
A swaying reed that any storm can break.
Come now, you have not seen us for so long,
Just try to spend one day with us. Don't go
930 To Altdorf, Uli. Hear? Don't go today.
Just give yourself, today, to your own people.

(*He takes his hand.*)

RUDENZ

I gave my word; I'm bound. Leave me alone.

ATTINGHAUSEN (*releasing his hand, speaking earnestly*)

Yes, you are surely bound, unlucky boy.
You're bound indeed, but not by word and oath;
You're tied securely by the bonds of love.   935

(RUDENZ *turns away*.)

Conceal it as you will, it is the Lady
Berta von Bruneck who draws you to the court
And chains you to the emperor and his service.
You think that you can win the noble lady
By leaving us. Do not deceive yourself.   940
She's held before you as a lure and snare,
But she's not destined for your innocence.

RUDENZ

Enough! I've heard enough. I'm going now.

(*Exit*.)

ATTINGHAUSEN

Stay here, my foolish boy! Well, he is gone.
I could not hold him back. I could not save him.   945
In this same way the bailiff Wolfenschiessen
Deserted us, and others will desert.
The foreign charm that's come into our mountains
Will draw away our youth with its allurements.
Oh, hour of grief, when strange and novel ways   950
Descended on our calm and happy valleys
And overturned our simple mode of life.
The new is sweeping in relentlessly;
The old gives way, and other times are coming.
Another race and other thoughts prevail.   955

Why am I here? They all are dead and buried,
With whom I lived and labored here so long.
My time is also buried. Fortunate
Is he who need not live to see the new.

(*Exit.*)

Scene II

A meadow surrounded by high cliffs and woods.

(*On the cliffs are paths with railings and ladders by which the countrymen later are seen descending. In the background appears the lake, over which a moon rainbow is seen as the scene begins. The view is closed by lofty mountains, behind which ice-covered peaks tower still higher. The scene is dark, but the lake and the white glaciers gleam in the moonlight.*)[5]

(Melchtal, Baumgarten, Winkelried, Meier von Sarnen, Burkhard am Bühel, Arnold von Sewa, Klaus von der Flüe, *and four other countrymen are arriving; all are armed.*)

Melchtal (*offstage*)

960   The pathway widens; quickly, follow me.
I know the mountain and the cross marked on it.
We've reached our goal. Here is the Rütli.

(*They enter with torches.*)

---

[5] The time is probably the night after the preceding scene, at 2:00 A.M., November 9, 1307.

WINKELRIED

Listen!

SEWA

All clear.

MEIER

There's no one here as yet. We men
Of Unterwalden are the first to come.

MELCHTAL

How late is it?

BAUMGARTEN

The watchman called out two   965
Just now, up in the town of Selisberg.

(The ringing of a bell is heard in the distance.)

MEIER

Be still!

AM BÜHEL

Across the lake in Schwyz the bells
Ring out for matins in the forest chapel.

VON DER FLÜE

The air is pure and bears the sound across.

MELCHTAL

Go gather brushwood, men, and light a fire,   970

That it may brightly burn to greet the others.

(*Two countrymen exit.*)

SEWA

It is a fair and glorious moonlit night.
The lake is calm and smooth, just like a mirror.

AM BÜHEL

They'll have an easy crossing now.

WINKELRIED (*pointing at the lake*)

But look!
975 Just look there! Don't you see it?

MEIER

What? Why, yes!
A rainbow in the middle of the night!

MELCHTAL

It is the moonlight that created it.

VON DER FLÜE

This is a wonderful and curious sign.
There're many men who never saw the like.

SEWA

980 It's double. Look, a paler one above it.

BAUMGARTEN

I see a boat that's passing right beneath it.

MELCHTAL

That must be Stauffacher and men from Schwyz.
He's prompt and doesn't make us wait for him.

(*He goes with* BAUMGARTEN *to the shore.*)

MEIER

The men from Uri are the slowest ones.

AM BÜHEL

They have to take a longer mountain path   985
In order to elude the viceroy's spies.

(*Meanwhile two countrymen have kindled a fire in
the middle of the site.*)

MELCHTAL (*on the shore*)

Who's there? Give us the word!

STAUFFACHER (*from below*)

                              Friends of our country.

(*All go upstage toward the newcomers.* STAUFFACHER,
ITEL REDING, HANS AUF DER MAUER, JÖRG IM HOFE, KON-
RAD HUNN, ULRICH DER SCHMIED, JOST VON WEILER *and
three other countrymen, all armed, come out of the boat.*)

ALL (*crying out*)

We welcome you!

(*While the others remain at the rear of the stage and
exchange greetings,* MELCHTAL *and* STAUFFACHER *come
forward.*)

MELCHTAL

                    My friend, I saw my father.
I saw the one who could not look at me.
990   I placed my hand upon his blinded eyes
And drew a burning impulse for revenge
From the extinguished sunlight of his face.

STAUFFACHER

Don't speak of vengeance. Don't avenge the past.
We want to fight the threat of future evil.
995   But tell me what you did in Unterwalden;
Say how you won adherents for our cause,
And what the people think, how you yourself
Escaped the snares of those who would betray you.

MELCHTAL

Across Surennen pass, through fearful mountains,
1000   And over vast and lonely fields of ice
Where only hungry birds of prey were croaking,
I reached the Alpine pastures, where the herdsmen
From Canton Uri and from Engelberg
Shout friendly greetings and graze their herds together.
1005   And as I went along I quenched my thirst
With glacier water flowing in the gullies,
Found lodging in the solitary huts,
Where I was host and guest alike, until
I came again to hospitable houses.
1010   Reports of the atrocity had spread
By then among all people in the valleys,
And my misfortune gained respect for me
At every door to which I went and knocked.
I found those good and honest men enraged
1015   About the tyranny of this regime.

Just as their pastures grow the selfsame plants
From year to year, and all their springs are flowing
Steadily, and even winds and clouds
Move in familiar paths across the sky,
So have the ancient customs stood unchanged   1020
From generation unto generation.
These people will not bear rash innovation
In the accustomed pattern of their lives.
They gave me willingly their hardened hands,
And from the walls took down their rusty swords;   1025
And in their eyes there shone a joyous courage
When I spoke out your name and Walter Fürst's,
Which are esteemed by every countryman.
They vowed to do whatever you might think
Was right and best, and swore to stand by you   1030
And faithfully to follow you till death.
I hurried on from farm to farm, protected
By sacred laws of hospitality.
And when I came into my native valley,
Where I have many kinsmen living near,   1035
And when I found my father, robbed and blind,
Compelled to live in strangers' homes, dependent
On others' charity—

STAUFFACHER

Merciful God!

MELCHTAL

I did not cry at all. I did not waste
The strength of burning grief in useless tears;   1040
I kept it as a treasure, deep and sure
Within my heart, and set my mind on action.
I wandered through the winding mountain paths

And searched out every isolated valley;
1045 Up to the icy edges of the glaciers
I looked for men and found them in their huts.
And in each place to which I came I found
The selfsame hatred of all tyranny;
For even to the highest boundaries
1050 Of vegetation, where the frozen soil
Refuses growth, the viceroy's greed has reached.
I stirred the spirits of these honest men,
Aroused them with my fiery, stinging words,
And they are on our side with all their hearts.

STAUFFACHER

1055 You have accomplished much in this short time.

MELCHTAL

That isn't all. The country people fear
The Rossberg and the Sarnen fortresses;
Secure behind their walls of stone, our foe
Finds safety while he ravages the land.
1060 With my own eyes I wanted to inspect them.
I went to Sarnen and surveyed the castle.

STAUFFACHER

You dared to go into the tiger's cave?

MELCHTAL

I went there well disguised in pilgrim's dress;
1065 Now judge yourself, do I have self-control?
I saw the viceroy revel at a feast.
I saw our foe and did not murder him.

STAUFFACHER

You surely had good luck in all your boldness.

(*Meanwhile the other countrymen have come forward, and they join the two.*)

But tell me now, who are these friends of yours,
These good and loyal men who followed you?
Let us be introduced, that we may speak   1070
With open hearts in trust and confidence.

MEIER

Who doesn't know you, sir, in all these lands?
My name in Meier von Sarnen, and this man is
My sister's son, named Struth von Winkelried.

STAUFFACHER

That is no unfamiliar name to me.   1075
It was a Winkelried who killed the dragon
Beside the Weiler swamp, and lost his life
In that great fight.

WINKELRIED

                    He was my grandfather.

MELCHTAL (*pointing at two countrymen*)

These two are workmen from the monastery
Of Engelberg. I hope you'll not reject them   1080
Because they're only bondsmen and can't live
As free men on their own inheritance.
They love the land, and everyone respects them.

STAUFFACHER (*to the two men*)

Give me your hands. Let him who is not bound
1085   Consider it good fortune for himself;
But honesty may thrive in any class.

KONRAD HUNN

This is Herr Reding, our former magistrate.

MEIER

I know him well. In court he's my opponent
In legal action for a piece of land.
1090   Herr Reding, we are enemies in court,
But here we are agreed.

(*He shakes Reding's hand.*)

STAUFFACHER

                              That's nobly said.

WINKELRIED

They're coming! Listen to the horn of Uri!

(*To the right and left, armed men are seen climbing down the cliffs with torches.*)

AUF DER MAUER

I see the reverend minister himself
Climb down the cliff with them. He spares no hardship
1095   And has no terror of the trip by night,
A faithful shepherd caring for his people.

BAUMGARTEN

I see the sacristan and Walter Fürst,
But I do not find Tell among the party.

(WALTER FÜRST, RÖSSELMANN *the pastor,* PETERMANN
the sacristan, KUONI *the herdsman,* WERNI *the hunter,*
RUODI *the fisherman, and five other countrymen enter.
The whole group of men, thirty-three in all, come forward
and take their places around the fire.*)

WALTER FÜRST

In secret we must meet on our own soil,
Which we obtained in freedom from our fathers,   1100
Convening furtively like murderers
At night, when darkness lends its cloak to crimes
And to conspirators who fear the light.
Thus must we seek out justice for ourselves—
A thing that is as pure and bright and fair   1105
As is the radiance of the light by day.

MELCHTAL

What's plotted in the darkness of the night
Shall joyfully and freely come to light.

RÖSSELMANN

Now hear, confederates, what God reveals.
We're meeting here instead of in assembly,   1110
And we can rightly represent the people.
So let us then hold session as is proper,
As we have always done in peaceful days;
And though the meeting is not strictly legal,

1115 These troubled times will surely sanction it.[6]
For God is surely there where justice rules,
And we're assembled underneath his heaven.

STAUFFACHER

Yes, let us hold our meeting by old custom.
Though it is night, our rights are clear as day.

MELCHTAL

1120 And if we're few, the hearts of all our people
Are with us here; the leaders are assembled.

KONRAD HUNN

Although we do not have our ancient books,
Their words have been engraved upon our hearts.

RÖSSELMANN

All right, let's form our circle, and in it plant
1125 Our swords as symbols of authority.

AUF DER MAUER

Now let our magistrate sit in his place,
With his two bailiffs standing at his side.

SACRISTAN

There are three cantons represented here.
To whom belongs the honor of presiding?

---

[6] The meeting is not legal because it is not public and is held at
night and without the statute books.

MEIER

Let Schwyz contest with Uri for this honor.   1130
We men from Unterwalden yield to you.

MELCHTAL

Yes, we will yield. We are the suppliants
Who're seeking help from you, our mighty friends.

STAUFFACHER

Then let the men from Uri take the sword;
Their banner led us when we went to Rome.[7]   1135

WALTER FÜRST

The honor of the sword should go to Schwyz,
For we are all descendants of that race.[8]

RÖSSELMANN

May I resolve the friendly competition?
In council Schwyz will lead; in battle, Uri.

WALTER FÜRST (*handing the swords to* STAUFFACHER)

Here, take them.

STAUFFACHER

                              No, to older men this honor.   1140

---

[7] The trips to Rome were made in order that the pope might
crown the newly elected German kings as Holy Roman emperors;
see lines 1231–1232.

[8] Tradition has it that Schwyz was settled first and gave the name
to all of Switzerland (*die Schweiz*); see lines 1167–1203.

IM HOFE

Ulrich der Schmied is oldest of us all.

AUF DER MAUER

He's brave indeed, but not a freeborn man.
A serf can't be a judge in Canton Schwyz.

STAUFFACHER

But here's Herr Reding, our former magistrate.
1145 Where could we find a more respected man?

WALTER FÜRST

Let him be magistrate and chairman here.
If you agree to this, raise up your hands.

(*All raise their right hands.*)

REDING (*stepping to the center*)

I cannot take my oath upon the books,
So I will swear by all the stars above
1150 That I will never turn aside from justice.

(*Two swords are set up before him. The circle is formed around him, Schwyz in the center, Uri to the right, and Unterwalden to the left. He stands leaning on his battle sword.*)

What is it that has brought the people here
From all these mountain cantons to assemble
At midnight on inhospitable shores?
What shall the purpose be of our new union
1155 That we establish here beneath the stars?

STAUFFACHER (*stepping into the circle*)

The union we establish is not new.
It is our fathers' ancient covenant
We now confirm. Mark well, confederates,
Although the lake, although the mountains part us,
And every canton rules itself at home,   1160
We're all one tribe and race, we're all one blood,
And all descendants of a common homeland.

WINKELRIED

Then it is true, as we have heard in songs,
Our fathers came from far into this land?
Please tell us everything you know, so that   1165
The old alliance makes the new one stronger.

STAUFFACHER

Then hear the tale the herdsmen tell each other.
There dwelt a mighty people in the north,
But they were struck by famine and hard times.
In this distress, the people's council voted   1170
That of the citizens one-tenth must leave
As chosen by the lot. And this was done.
The men and women left with lamentation,
A mighty host of people going south,
And fought their way across the German lands   1175
Up to the highlands of these forest mountains.
The great migration did not stop or tire
Until they came into the lonely valley
Where now the Muotta flows across the meadows.
Here they could see no trace of human life   1180
Except a hut that stood beside the lake.

There sat a man who tended an old ferry.[9]
But since the surging lake could not be crossed,
They looked around, surveyed the pleasant land,
1185 And saw there an abundance of fine timber;
Soon they discovered springs that flowed good water.
So they were satisfied and felt at home,
And they resolved to settle in that place.
They founded there the ancient town of Schwyz,
1190 And many days were filled with bitter struggles
As they dug out entangled roots of forests.
And when the soil no longer could support
The many people living there, they moved
On farther to the forest-covered mountains,
1195 And reached the fields of snow, beyond whose walls
Another people speak another language.
They built the town of Stanz beside the Kernwald,
And Altdorf in the valley of the Reuss.
But always they remembered their beginnings.
1200 From all the foreign tribes who later settled
Inside their borders and within their midst,[10]
The men of Schwyz can recognize each other;
Their hearts, their blood, will make themselves be known.

(*He stretches out his hands to the right and left.*)

AUF DER MAUER

Yes, we are one in heart and one in blood!

---

[9] The contradiction between the man at the ferry and "no trace of
human life" is found in the folk songs.

[10] Other Teutonic tribes such as the Franks, the Burgundians, and
some of the Goths.

ALL (*clasping each other's hands*)

Yes, one we are, and we shall act together.   1205

STAUFFACHER

The other nations bear a foreign yoke
Because they yielded to the conqueror,
And even some within our country's borders
Are serfs who still bear foreign obligations.
Their bondage is transmitted to their children.   1210
But we, who are the true and ancient Swiss,
Have always treasured and preserved our freedom.
We did not bend our knees before the princes;
We freely chose the emperor's protection.

RÖSSELMANN

We freely chose the Empire's shield and shelter;   1215
It's written so in Emperor Frederick's grant.

STAUFFACHER

For even free men have an overlord.
There must be government, a highest judge,
To render justice when there are disputes;
And in their lands, which they had wrested from   1220
The wilderness, our fathers gladly gave
This honor to the emperor, who's called
The lord of Germany and Italy.
And like the other free men of his realm
They pledged themselves to military service,   1225
For this must be the freeman's only duty:
To shield the realm that is his own defense.

MELCHTAL

And anything beyond would mark the slave.

STAUFFACHER

And when the army summons came, they joined
1230 The royal banners and fought the kingdom's wars.
They went along to Italy in armor
To place the Roman crown upon his head.
But they were free to rule themselves at home
According to their laws and ancient customs;
1235 The kaiser's only right was penal justice.
For this he named some great and noble count
Whose residence was in another land.
When murder cases came, they called him in,
And under clear and open skies he stood
1240 And fearlessly he spoke his rightful verdict.
What traces do you find of serfdom here?
If any of you disagrees, speak out.

IM HOFE

No. Everything is just as you have said.
We never tolerated despotism.

STAUFFACHER

1245 And we refused obedience to the kaiser
When he abused our rights to help the priests.
For when Einsiedeln monastery's men
Laid claim to pastures that belonged to us,
Which we had used for grazing many years,
1250 And when the abbot then produced a letter
That gave the unclaimed wilderness to him
(For our existence there had been suppressed),

We said, "That letter was obtained by fraud!
No emperor can give away what's ours;
And if we get no justice in the Empire,   1255
We'll do without the Empire in our mountains."
Thus spoke our fathers then. How can we now
Endure the shamefulness of this new yoke
And tolerate from foreign underlings
The things that emperors don't dare to do?   1260
This soil we have created for ourselves
By our own hands and by our diligence.
The woods that were the wild abode of bears
We have transformed for human habitation;
We drained the swamps to kill the dragon's brood   1265
That sent out pestilence and noxious vapors; [11]
We tore apart the shroud of mist that hung
In constant gray about this wilderness;
We broke the rock, and for the wanderer
We built a sturdy bridge across the gorge.   1270
This soil is ours by a thousand years' possession.
And shall some foreign lord, himself a vassal,
Now dare to come and fasten us in chains
And put us to disgrace on our own soil?
Is there no help against such harsh oppression?   1275

> (*There is a great commotion among the country-
> men.*)

There must be limits to such tyranny:
When the oppressed can find no justice here,
And when his burdens grow unbearable,
He'll reach with confidence right up to heaven
And draw from there his everlasting rights,   1280

---

[11] Another dragon story, as in line 1076, but this time Schiller
makes dragon-killing symbolic of the draining of the swamps.

Which still abide on high, inalienable
And indestructible as are the stars.
The ancient state of nature now returns,
When man stands face to face with hostile man;
1285 And as a last resort, when nothing else
Avails, he has his sword to draw in battle.
It is our dearest treasures we defend
Against oppression. We'll stand for our own land,
We'll stand for our own homes, our wives and children.

ALL (*clashing their swords*)

1290 We'll stand for our own homes, our wives and children

RÖSSELMANN (*stepping into the circle*)

Before you draw the sword, consider well
That you might make a peaceful compromise.
It costs you but one word, and soon the tyrants,
Who now oppress, will coax and flatter you.
1295 Accept what they have often offered you;
Renounce the Empire, swear to Austria.

AUF DER MAUER

What are you saying? Swear to Austria!

AM BÜHEL

Don't listen, men!

WINKELRIED

A traitor counsels this,
Our country's foe!

Reding

        Be still, confederates!

Sewa

Give homage in disgrace to Austria? 1300

Von der Flüe

Let them extort from us by violence
What we denied to kindness?

Meier

            Then we'd be,
And would deserve to be, no more than slaves.

Auf der Mauer

Let us expel from rights in Switzerland
Whoever wants to yield to Austria. 1305
I stand on this and I demand it, chairman.
Let it become the first new law we make.

Melchtal

So be it, then. Whoever speaks of yielding
To Austria shall lose his rights and honor.
And let no man receive him in his home. 1310

All (*raising their right hands*)

Agreed. Let this be law.

Reding (*after a pause*)

        It is the law.

RÖSSELMANN

Now you are free; by this new law you're free.
The Austrians shall not extort by force
What they did not obtain by friendly means.

JOST VON WEILER

1315 Proceed with business now.

REDING

                    Confederates,
Has every gentle means been sought and tried?
Perhaps the emperor has never known,
Perhaps it's not his will that we should suffer.
We must attempt this last resort as well,
1320 And lay our grievances before his throne
Before we take up swords. For horrible
Is violence, although the cause is just.
God only helps when men can help no more.

STAUFFACHER (*to* KONRAD HUNN)

Now you must speak and give us your report.

KONRAD HUNN

1325 I was in Rheinfeld at the kaiser's palace
To lodge complaints against the viceroys' acts
And claim our covenant of ancient freedom,
Which every king confirmed when he took office.
I found the envoys there from many cities,
1330 From Swabia and lands along the Rhine;
They all received the charters they requested,
And they returned well pleased to their own lands.
But they sent me, your envoy, to advisers,

Who sent me on with empty consolations.
They said the kaiser had no time right now;   1335
Another day he might consider us.
And as I walked in sadness through the halls,
I saw Duke John of Swabia stand weeping
Beside a balcony, and round him stood
The noble lords of Wart and Tegerfeld,   1340
Who called to me and said: "Defend yourselves!
You'll get no justice from the emperor.
Does he not rob his own dear brother's child,
Withhold from him his just inheritance?
The duke is asking for his mother's share;   1345
His plea is that he is of age and now
It's time for him to rule his land and people.
What answer did he get? The kaiser placed
A wreath on him—'to ornament his youth.' "

Auf der Mauer

You've heard it now. Do not expect the kaiser   1350
To grant us rights. We must defend ourselves.

Reding

We have no other course. Now let us plan
A strategy by which we might succeed.

Walter Fürst (*stepping into the circle*)

We want to drive away despised oppression,
And thus preserve the ancient rights and freedom   1355
That were our fathers' legacy to us,
But we'll not reach for new things unrestrained.
We'll render unto Caesar what is Caesar's.
Who has a lord should render faithful service.

MEIER

1360 I hold my land in fief from Austria.

WALTER FÜRST

Continue to discharge your feudal duties.

JOST VON WEILER

I pay my dues to the lords of Rappersweil.

WALTER FÜRST

Continue to remit your tithes and taxes.

RÖSSELMANN

I am a vassal of Our Lady of Zurich.

WALTER FÜRST

1365 Then render to the cloister what's the cloister's.

STAUFFACHER

I hold my land directly from the Empire.

WALTER FÜRST

We'll do what must be done, but nothing more!
We'll drive away the viceroys and their soldiers,
Attack the fortresses and break them down;
1370 But if it's possible, let's shed no blood.
The king shall see that only through compulsion
Do we cast off our sacred duties to him.
And if he sees us act with due restraint,
Perhaps he'll wisely overcome his anger;
1375 For any nation gains a just respect

If it restrains itself with sword in hand.

REDING

But let us hear. How shall we manage it?
Our enemy has weapons in his hand,
And surely he will never yield in peace.

STAUFFACHER

He will when he has seen us with our weapons.   1380
We'll take him by surprise before he's ready.

MEIER

That is far easier said than it is done.
Two mighty fortresses stand in our country;
They'll shield our enemy and threaten us
If ever royal troops invade our country.   1385
Rossberg and Sarnen castles must be taken
Before we draw the sword in our three cantons.

STAUFFACHER

If you delay that long, our foe is warned.
There are too many men who share our secret.

MEIER

There are no traitors in these forest cantons.   1390

RÖSSELMANN

Our very zeal, though good, can well betray us.

WALTER FÜRST

If we delay, the Uri fortress will
Be finished and the governor secure.

MEIER

You're thinking of yourselves.

SACRISTAN

                 And *you're* unjust.

MEIER (*starting up*)

1395   Unjust? Can Uri men say that to us?

REDING

Be quiet, by your oath.

MEIER

                 All right, if Schwyz
Agrees with Uri, we must indeed be silent.

REDING

I must reproach you in the assembly's name,
For you disturb our peace with words of anger.
1400   Don't we all stand united for one cause?

WINKELRIED

Let us postpone it until Christmas time,
When, by our custom, all the serfs will come
To Sarnen castle to bring the viceroy gifts;
Then ten or twelve of our confederates
1405   Can meet without suspicion in the castle.
They'll take along some spearheads secretly,
Which they can quickly fasten to their staffs,
For no one gets into the castle armed.
A larger troop will wait in nearby woods;

Then, when the men inside have seized the gates, 1410
They'll blow a horn to signal for the charge,
And those in ambush will attack in force.
The castle will be ours with little effort.

MELCHTAL

I'll undertake to climb up Rossberg's walls.
One of the castle maids is fond of me, 1415
And I'll persuade her easily to lower
A light rope ladder for a nighttime visit.
And once I'm in, I'll pull my friends up too.

REDING

Is it your will that we should put it off?

(*The majority raise their hands.*)

STAUFFACHER (*counting the votes*)

A count of twenty for, and twelve against! 1420

WALTER FÜRST

And when the castles fall as we have planned,
We'll send our signals out with smoke and fire
From mountaintop to mountaintop. The call
To arms will be proclaimed in every town.
And when the governors have seen us armed, 1425
Believe me, they will gladly quit the fight
And readily accept a peaceful escort
In order to escape beyond our borders.

STAUFFACHER

But I'm afraid that Gessler will resist us.
He is protected by his dreaded troopers; 1430

He will not yield without first shedding blood.
Although he's driven out, he'll threaten us.
It's rash and almost dangerous to spare him.

BAUMGARTEN

Wherever it is dangerous, send *me!*
1435 I owe my life to Tell—he rescued me—
And I will risk it gladly for my country.
Thus I appease my heart and guard my honor.

REDING

With time comes wisdom. We must wait in patience.
Some things are best decided at the moment.
1440 But look, while we are meeting here by night,
The morning dawns upon the highest mountains
And sets its beacon lights above. Let's leave
Before the light of day surprises us.

WALTER FÜRST

Don't fear. The night leaves slowly from the valleys.

(*All have removed their hats and are watching the
breaking of dawn in quiet meditation.*)

RÖSSELMANN

1445 By this new light that greets us first, before
All other people living far below
Where they must breathe the stale air of the towns,
Let us now swear the oath of our new union.
We want to be a nation of true brothers,
1450 And stand as one in danger and distress.

(*They all repeat his words with three fingers raised.*)

We will be free, just as our fathers were,
And we will die before we'll live as slaves.

> (*They all repeat as before.*)

We want to place our trust in God most high,
And never fear the might of mortal man.

> (*They all repeat again and embrace each other.*)

STAUFFACHER

Now let each man go calmly on his way   1455
To his own friends and his community.
Whoever is a herdsman, tend your herds
And quietly win friends for our new union.
Endure what you must suffer until then,
And let the tyrants' debts to us increase   1460
Until the day of reckoning is here,
And they must pay those debts to each and all.
Let everyone restrain his righteous rage
And hold his vengeance back, to serve the whole;
For if one man thinks only of himself,   1465
He robs our common welfare and our goal.

> (*As they go away in three different directions in profound silence, the orchestra strikes up a splendid flourish. The empty stage remains open for a while and shows the spectacle of the sun rising above the glaciers.*)

ACT THREE

SCENE I

The yard in front of TELL's *house.*[1]

(TELL *is busy with his ax, and* HEDWIG, *his wife, is engaged in housework.* WALTER *and* WILHELM *are playing with a small crossbow in the background.*)

WALTER (*singing*)

With his bow and arrow
Over hill and vale
Strides the fearless hunter
1470   Early on the trail.

As the soaring eagle
Rules his wide domain,
So among the mountains
Does the hunter reign.

1475   His is all the vastness
Where his arrows strike;
His is all the quarry,
Bird and beast alike.[2]

---

[1] Tell's house is in Bürglen, Uri, and the date is apparently November 20, 1307.

[2] Robert Schumann set Walter's song to music in "The Boy Archer's Song" (Opus 79, No. 25, 1849). There is also a setting by B. A. Weber, "The Archer."

(*He comes running.*)

My string is broken. Fix it for me, Father.

TELL

Not I. A real hunter helps himself.   1480

(*The boys withdraw.*)

HEDWIG

The boys are starting young to take up shooting.

TELL

This early practice makes for mastery.

HEDWIG

I wish to God they wouldn't learn at all.

TELL

They should learn everything, and learn it well.
Whoever wants to make his way through life   1485
Must be prepared.

HEDWIG

          And neither one will be
Content to stay at home.

TELL

            I can't be either.
I was not born to be a herdsman, Hedwig;
I always have to chase some fleeting goal,

1490 And only can enjoy my life completely
When I must work to win it every day.[3]

HEDWIG

But you are not concerned about my fears—
How I may worry, waiting here for you;
For I am terrified at what they tell
1495 About your daring trips and risky ventures.
At each farewell my trembling heart is sure
That you will not come back to me again.
I see you lost in wild and icy mountains,
Or failing in your leap from crag to crag;
1500 I see the frightened chamois jumping back
To drag you down with him into the gorge;
I see you buried by an avalanche;
I see the glacier's treacherous abyss
Split under you, and see you falling down,
1505 Interred alive in such a dreadful grave!
For death, in a hundred changing forms, pursues
And snatches at the daring Alpine hunter.
Yours is indeed a miserable calling
That takes you to the very brink of death.

TELL

1510 Whoever looks around with open eyes
And trusts in God and his own ready strength
Can keep himself from danger and distress.
He fears no mountains who was born among them.

---

[3] Compare Goethe's *Faust,* Part II, lines 11,575–11,576: "He only earns his freedom and existence, / Who daily conquers them anew" (tr. Bayard Taylor [Boston: Houghton Mifflin Company, 1870], II, 294).

(*He has finished his work and lays aside his tools.*)

I think that gate will last a good long time.
An ax at home will save the carpenter.   1515

    (*He takes his hat.*)

    HEDWIG

Where are you going?

    TELL

                To Altdorf, to your father.

    HEDWIG

You're up to something dangerous. What is it?

    TELL

What gave you such a thought?

    HEDWIG

                    I hear of plots
Against the governors. There was a meeting
Held at the Rütli. You were at it too.   1520

    TELL

I wasn't there; but when my country calls,
I'll not hold back, or hesitate to serve.

    HEDWIG

They'll put you where the danger is the greatest.
Your task will be the hardest one, as always.

TELL

1525   We'll all be taxed according to our talents.

HEDWIG

There was that Underwalden man you took
Across the lake—it was a miracle
That you escaped. And did you never think
Of wife and children then?

TELL

                    I thought of you.
1530   That's why I saved that father for his children.

HEDWIG

To venture out on such tempestuous seas—
I call that tempting God, not trusting him.

TELL

Who thinks too long will not accomplish much.

HEDWIG

You're kind and friendly, helping everyone,
1535   But there'll be none to help when you're in trouble.

TELL

God grant that I may never need their help.

(*He takes up his crossbow and arrows.*)

HEDWIG

Why do you take your bow? Just leave it here.

TELL

My arm is missing when I am without it.

(*The boys return.*)

WALTER

Where are you going, Father?

TELL

                    To Altdorf, Son,
To Granddad. Do you want to come?

WALTER

                         Of course!   1540

HEDWIG

The governor is there. Don't go to Altdorf.

TELL

He'll leave today.

HEDWIG

                    Then wait until he's gone.
He bears a grudge against us; don't remind him.

TELL

His malice isn't apt to injure me.
I do what's right and fear no enemy.   1545

HEDWIG

Those who do right are just the men he hates.

TELL

Because he cannot touch them. So I think
This knight will surely let me go in peace.

HEDWIG

Are you so sure of that?

TELL

Not long ago
1550 I was out hunting in the wild ravines
Of Schächen Valley, on deserted trails.
A precipice rose high and steep above me,
While down below the Schächen River roared.
And as I walked alone upon a ledge
1555 Too narrow for a man to step aside,

(*The boys press close on his right and left and look
up at him with eager curiosity.*)

There coming toward me was the governor,
Alone as I, and thus we faced each other,
Just man to man, with the abyss below.
And when his lordship found me there before him,
1560 And recognized me as the man he'd punished
Severely for slight cause not long before,
And when he saw me with my stately weapon
Come striding up to him, his face turned pale,
His knees gave way, and I began to think
1565 That he would fall unconscious down the cliff.
I pitied him, so I stepped up to him
And just said modestly, "It's I, your Lordship."
But he could never bring a single word
To pass his lips, and so he raised his hand
1570 And dumbly motioned me to go away.
Then I went on and sent him his attendants.

HEDWIG

He trembled there before you; that is bad.
He'll not forgive you that you saw him weak.

TELL

I shun him now, and he won't look for me.

HEDWIG

Then stay away from there today; go hunting. 1575

TELL

What has come over you?

HEDWIG

I am afraid.

TELL

How can you be so worried without reason?

HEDWIG

Because I have no reason. Tell, stay here!

TELL

I gave my word that I'd be there today.

HEDWIG

Well, if you must, then go—but leave the boy. 1580

WALTER

No, Mother, I'm going along with Father.

HEDWIG

But Walter, surely you won't leave your mother.

WALTER

I'll bring you something pretty back from Granddad.

(*He leaves with his father.*)

WILHELM

See, Mother, I will stay with you.

HEDWIG (*embracing him*)

You are
1585 My precious child, and you are all I have.

(*She goes to the yard gate and looks with anxious eyes after the two who are leaving.*)

SCENE II

A forest surrounded by cliffs, from which water falls in fine spray.[4]

(BERTA *enters in hunting dress,* RUDENZ *following her.*)

BERTA

He's following me. Here is my chance to speak.

---

[4] The setting is near Altdorf, and the time seems to be about the same as in the previous scene (November 20, 1307).

Schiller meant to give this scene a lyrical tone. This accounts for the rhymes at the beginning and again later in the scene. Most of these rhymes were retained in the translation for the same reason.

RUDENZ (*enters hurriedly*)

At last, my lady, we are all alone,
Surrounded by a precipice of stone.
No one can hear us in this wilderness.
I'll break this endless silence, and profess—   1590

BERTA

But are you sure the hunt won't follow us? [5]

RUDENZ

The hunting party went in that direction.
It's now or never; I must use this moment.
I want to hear my fate decided now,
Though it should mean that I must give you up.   1595
But do not fortify your gentle eyes
With such a stern expression! Who am I
To look at you with bold and hopeful thoughts?
I have achieved no fame; I cannot yet
Be numbered with the noble knights who come,   1600
Renowned in victory, to pay you court,
While I bring only love and loyalty.

BERTA (*earnestly and with severity*)

How can you speak of love and loyalty—
You who are faithless in your closest duties?

(RUDENZ *steps back.*)

The slave of Austria, who sells himself   1605
To foreigners, oppressors of his people?

---

[5] This is Gessler's hunting expedition, from which he returns in
the next scene.

RUDENZ

From you, my lady, must I hear this censure?
Whom was I seeking on that side but you?

BERTA

You thought to find me on the side of treason?
1610 No, I would rather give my hand to Gessler,
The tyrant and oppressor of our land,
Than to a son of Switzerland who turns
A renegade and is the tyrant's tool.

RUDENZ

Oh God, what must I hear?

BERTA

                                        Just tell me then,
1615 What's closer to a man than his own people?
What finer duties for a noble heart
Than the protection of the innocent
And the defense of those who are oppressed?
My heart is bleeding for your patient people;
1620 I suffer with them, for I've come to love them
Because they are so modest in their strength.
My mind and soul are drawn to them completely,
And every day I must esteem them higher.
But you, whom nature and your knightly duties
1625 Have marked to be their natural defender,
You who forsake them, join the enemy
And forge the fetters for your native land—
It's you who hurt and grieve me, and I must
Restrain my heart to keep from hating you.

RUDENZ

Am I not thinking of my people's welfare?　　　　　　1630
Beneath the scepter of the Austrians
There's peace—

BERTA

　　　　　　　What you prepare for them is serfdom.
You'd drive out freedom from the final stronghold
That's left to it on earth. The people know
Much better where their true advantage lies;　　　　1635
They're not misled by false appearances.
But you've been caught; you're taken in the net.

RUDENZ

You surely hate me, Berta. You despise me.

BERTA

I wish I could; that would be better. But now—
To see the one I'd like to love despised,　　　　　1640
To see him worthy of contempt—

RUDENZ

　　　　　　　　　　　Oh, Berta!
You let me catch a glimpse of heavenly bliss
And that same moment fling me down the abyss.

BERTA

Your noble qualities are not yet stifled;
They are asleep. I want to wake them up.　　　　　1645
I think that you have tried, by force of will,
To kill the innate goodness of your heart,

But it is mightier than you yourself.
In spite of all, I see you're good and noble.

RUDENZ

1650 You still have faith in me! Believe me, Berta,
Your love can make me be and do all things.

BERTA

Just be what nature destined you to be.
Fulfill the duties she assigned to you,
By standing with your people and your country
1655 To fight for justice and your sacred rights.

RUDENZ

How can I win you, have you as my own,
If I resist the power of the kaiser?
Don't your own kinfolk rule your hand and fate
According to their powerful designs?

BERTA

1660 My own estates lie in these forest cantons,
And if the Swiss are free, then I am free.

RUDENZ

Oh, what a prospect you have opened up!

BERTA

Don't hope to win me by a Hapsburg favor.
They're stretching out their hands for my possessions,
1665 Which they intend to join to their great holdings.
The greed for land that would devour your freedom
Is threatening to take my freedom too.

Yes, I have been selected as a victim
To be bestowed upon some favorite;
They want to drag me to the royal court,   1670
Where intrigue rules, deceit of every sort.
There hateful marriage fetters wait for me,
And only love, your love, can set me free.

RUDENZ

Could you decide to spend your lifetime here
And be my own, in my own fatherland?   1675
What was my yearning after distant places
Except my striving to be near to you?
For you were what I sought on paths of glory,
And my ambition was but love for you.
If you could isolate yourself with me   1680
In this calm land, resigning worldly splendor,
Then I would reach the end of all my striving;
Then let the waters of the troubled world
Surge up against the mountain shores around us.
I have no further transient desires   1685
To search for in the distant realms of life.
Now may these rocky cliffs spread far and wide
Impenetrable walls on every side;
May this enclosed and blissful valley be
Illumined from above for you and me.   1690

BERTA

Now you are what my hoping heart surmised
And dreamed about. My faith did not deceive me.

RUDENZ

Now leave me, vain delusion that beguiled me.
I'll find my happiness in my own home.

1695 Here where I spent my boyhood joyfully,
      Where thousands of bright memories surround me,
      Where springs and trees have come to life around me,
      In our own fatherland, you will be mine.
      I've always loved this country of my birth;
1700 I'd long for it through all the joys of earth.

          BERTA

      Where could we ever find the Blessed Isles
      If not in this fair land of innocence?
      Here where the ancient loyalties yet live,
      Where falsehood still has never found its way,
1705 No envy can obscure our happiness;
      The hours will pass and fill each shining day.
      In true and manly worth I see you there,
      The first among these free and equal men;
      You'll be revered with homage, and you'll share
1710 The privilege of king and citizen.

          RUDENZ

      I see you there, the queen of womankind,
      In charming feminine activity.
      You'll make my home a heaven and I'll find
      That as the flowers of spring adorn the lea,
1715 So will your life and charms adorn me too,
      And everything will always thrive near you.

          BERTA

      You see, Rudenz, why I was sad and worried
      When I saw you destroy your happiness
      Yourself. I thought of what my fate would be
1720 If I should have to marry the oppressor
      And follow him into his gloomy castle.

There is no fortress here. There are no walls
To part me from a people I would help.

RUDENZ

How can I save myself, how break the noose
Which foolishly I placed around my neck?   1725

BERTA

Just tear it off with brave determination.
Whatever comes, stand firmly by your people.
That is where you belong.

(*Hunting horns are heard in the distance.*)

                                        I hear the hunt
Come near. Let's go; we'll have to leave each other.
Fight for your fatherland and fight for love.   1730
There is one foe before whose might we tremble;
There is one freedom that will free us all.

(*Exeunt.*)

SCENE III

A meadow near Altdorf.[6]

(*In the foreground are trees; in the background, the hat
on a pole. The view is bounded by the Bannberg, over
which snow-covered mountains tower.*)

---

[6] The setting "near Altdorf" disagrees with the crier's earlier
proclamation "in Altdorf" (line 395) and the suggestion of a *Platz*
or plaza which the people cross when coming from the town hall
(lines 1740–1744). Tradition sets the locale on the town square of
Altdorf. Schiller may have been influenced by old woodcuts that
show the apple-shooting near the town.

FRIESSHARD *and* LEUTHOLD *are standing guard.*

FRIESSHARD

We keep our watch in vain. No one will come
This way and pay his homage to the hat.
1735　It used to be just like a fair out here,
But now the village green is all deserted
Since they have hung this scarecrow on the pole.

LEUTHOLD

Yes, only riffraff lets itself be seen
And, just to vex us, doffs those ragged caps.
1740　All decent people turn away and take
A long detour halfway around the town
To keep from bowing down before the hat.

FRIESSHARD

Some people had to cross this place at noon
When they were coming from a town-hall meeting,
1745　So I was sure I'd make a catch, because
Their minds were far from greeting any hat.
But Rösselmann the priest, who just then came
From visiting a sick man, saw it all
And held the Host [7] up high before the pole.
1750　The sacristan then had to ring his bell,
And all fell on their knees—including me—
And reverenced the Host, but not the hat.

LEUTHOLD

Look here, Friesshard, it seems to me sometimes
As if we're standing in the pillory.

---

[7] The Eucharistic wafer used in the sacrament of the Lord's Supper.

It surely is a shame for any trooper   1755
To stand on guard before an empty hat,
And every decent fellow must despise us.
To tell the truth, it is a foolish order
To ask that men pay homage to a hat.

FRIESSHARD

Why not pay homage to a hollow hat?   1760
You've often bowed before a hollow skull.

(HILDEGARD, MECHTHILD, *and* ELSBET *enter with
their children and stand around the pole.*)

LEUTHOLD

I tell you, you are one officious scoundrel
Who'd like to get good people into trouble.
Let those who will walk by before the hat;
I'll close my eyes or look the other way.   1765

MECHTHILD

There hangs the governor. Pay homage, boys.

ELSBET

I wish to God he'd go, and leave his hat.
Our country wouldn't be the worse for it.

FRIESSHARD (*driving them away*)

Get out of here! Confounded pack of women!
Who sent for you? Go home and send your husbands,   1770
If they have courage to defy the order.

(*The women leave.*)

(TELL *enters with his crossbow, leading his son by the hand. They walk past the hat without noticing it and go toward the front of the stage.*)

WALTER (*pointing at the Bannberg*)

Say, Father, is it true the trees up there
Upon the mountain bleed if someone strikes
Them with an ax?

TELL

                        Who says such things, my boy?

WALTER

1775 The master herdsman told us; and he said
The trees were all enchanted, and the hand
That injured them would grow out from the grave.[8]

TELL

The trees are all enchanted, that is true.
You see the glaciers there, the icy peaks
1780 That fade away and melt into the sky?

WALTER

Those are the peaks that thunder in the night
And send the avalanches down the mountains.

---

[8] The superstition about the trees is apparently derived from the word *Bannberg* itself. The German verb *bannen* has a double meaning: "to be charmed, enchanted," and "to protect by law, put under the ban." Folklore prefers the idea of enchantment, but actually the trees *protect* the town from avalanches, as Tell points out.

TELL

That's right, and they would long ago have covered
The little town of Altdorf with their mass
If those same forests were not standing there,   1785
A mighty bulwark for our town's protection.

WALTER (*after thinking a while*)

And are there countries with no mountains, Father?

TELL

If you go down from our high mountain peaks,
Keep going lower as the rivers run,
You'll reach a great and level piece of land   1790
Where forest streams no longer rush and foam,
And rivers calmly flow in beds of sand.
There all around you is the heaven's dome,
And you will see the fertile fields of grain
Spread out like garden spots across the plain.   1795

WALTER

But Father, why don't we go down at once
And live in this fine land you talk about,
Instead of staying here with so much worry?

TELL

The land is fair and gracious like the heavens;
But they who till the soil do not enjoy   1800
The crops that they have planted.

WALTER

                                                 Don't they live
As free as you upon their own possessions?

TELL

The bishop and the king own all the land.

WALTER

But surely they go hunting in the forests?

TELL

1805   The overlord owns all the hunting rights.

WALTER

But surely they go fishing in the rivers?

TELL

The king owns all the streams, the seas, the salt.

WALTER

Who is this king that everybody fears?

TELL

He is the one who guards and feeds them all.

WALTER

1810   But aren't they brave? Why can't they guard themselves?

TELL

No neighbor dares to trust his neighbor there.

WALTER

Oh, Father, I'd feel cramped in that wide land.
I'd rather live beneath the avalanche.

TELL

It's better to have glaciers at your back,
My son, than evil men whom you can't trust.   1815

(*They are about to pass by.*)

WALTER

Look, Father, see the hat hung on the pole.

TELL

What is the hat to us? Come, let's go on.

(*As he is about to leave,* FRIESSHARD *approaches him
with leveled pike.*)

FRIESSHARD

By the kaiser's orders, halt! I tell you, halt!

TELL (*laying hold of the pike*)

What do you want? Why are you stopping me?

FRIESSHARD

You've disobeyed the order. Come with us.   1820

LEUTHOLD

You failed to pay your homage to the hat.

TELL

Friend, let me go.

FRIESSHARD

> Away with him to prison.

WALTER

My father go to prison? Help! Help!

(*He calls toward the wings.*)

Come quickly, people! Someone come and help!
1825 They'll capture him and take him off to prison!

> (RÖSSELMANN *the priest and* PETERMANN *the sacris-
> tan enter, with three other men.*)

SACRISTAN

What's happening?

RÖSSELMANN

> Why did you seize this man?

FRIESSHARD

He is the kaiser's enemy, a traitor.

TELL (*seizing him violently*)

A traitor, I?

RÖSSELMANN

> You're wrong, my friend. This man
Is Tell, an honest, loyal citizen.

WALTER (*seeing* WALTER FÜRST *and running up to
him*)

1830 Grandfather, help! They want to take my father.

FRIESSHARD

Away to prison!

WALTER FÜRST (*hurrying forward*)

Wait, I'll offer bail.
For heaven's sake, what's happened to you, Tell?

(MELCHTAL *and* STAUFFACHER *enter.*)

FRIESSHARD

He has despised the viceroy's sovereign power,
And still refuses to acknowledge it.

STAUFFACHER

You claim that Tell did that?

MELCHTAL

You're lying, fellow.   1835

LEUTHOLD

He did not pay his homage to the hat.

WALTER FÜRST

And just for that you're taking him to prison?
Here, friend, accept my bail and set him free.

FRIESSHARD

You'd better keep your bail to save yourself.
We're doing our duty here. Away with him!   1840

MELCHTAL (*to the people*)

This is outrageous wrong. Shall we endure it,
And let them drag him off before our eyes?

SACRISTAN

We are the stronger. Friends, do not allow this.
We'll stand as one and back each other up.

FRIESSHARD

1845 Who dares resist the governor's command?

THREE OTHER COUNTRYMEN (*running in*)

We'll help you. What has happened? Knock them down!

(HILDEGARD, MECHTHILD *and* ELSBET *return*.)

TELL

Go on, good people, I can help myself.
Don't think, if I should want to use my strength,
That I would ever fear those pikes of theirs.

MELCHTAL (*to* FRIESSHARD)

1850 Just dare to take this man away from us.

WALTER FÜRST *and* STAUFFACHER

Calm down. Stay quiet.

FRIESSHARD (*screaming*)

         Riot and rebellion!

(*Hunting horns are heard.*)

WOMEN

Here comes the viceroy.

FRIESSHARD (*raising his voice*)

Mutiny! Rebellion!

STAUFFACHER

Scream till you burst, you scoundrel!

RÖSSELMANN *and* MELCHTAL

Keep still, can't you?

FRIESSHARD (*screaming louder*)

Help us! Help the servants of the law!

WALTER FÜRST

The governor! What will he do to us?   1855

(*Enter* GESSLER, *on horseback and holding a falcon on his fist,* RUDOLF DER HARRAS, BERTA, *and* RUDENZ, *with a large train of armed attendants who form a circle of pikes around the whole stage.*)

RUDOLF DER HARRAS

Make way there for his lordship!

GESSLER

Disperse the crowd!
Why are they gathered here? Who called for help?

(*General silence*)

Who was it? I want to know who called.

(*To* FRIESSHARD)

                                        Come here!
Say who you are and why you hold this man.

(*He gives the falcon to a servant.*)

FRIESSHARD

1860   My noble lord, I am your man-at-arms,
        Your soldier, duly named to guard the hat.
        This man I apprehended in the act
        Of passing by the hat without obeisance.
        I started to arrest him as you ordered,
1865   But now the crowd would rescue him by force.

        GESSLER (*after a pause*)

        Look, Tell, do you despise your kaiser so,
        And me, who rule as viceroy in his place,
        That you refuse your homage to the hat
        Which I put up to test obedience here?
1870   You have revealed to me your bad intentions.

        TELL

        Forgive me, sir. It was through oversight,
        And not contempt for you, that this thing happened.
        Were I discreet, my name would not be Tell.[9]
        I ask your mercy. I'll not offend again.

_____

    [9] There have been various attempts to explain the name Tell. One
theory would associate the word with the German *toll* ("mad, crazy")
and the English cognate "dull"; another (by Grimm), with the Latin
telum ("arrow"). Here Schiller follows Tschudi, who inferred some
such attribute as foolishness, simplicity, or lack of discretion. See also
lines 443–446, where Tell is depicted as a plain man of action rather
than a reflective person. Cf. lines 1904–1910.

GESSLER (*after a silence*)

You are a master with the crossbow, Tell.   1875
They say you are a match for any archer.

WALTER TELL

And that's the truth, sir. Father shoots an apple
Right off the tree, a hundred steps away.

GESSLER

Your son, I take it, Tell?

TELL

                                        Yes, noble lord.

GESSLER

Is this your only child?

TELL

                                        I have two boys.   1880

GESSLER

And of the two, which one do you love more?

TELL

Both boys are dear to me alike, my lord.

GESSLER

Look, Tell, because they say you shoot an apple
Down from the tree a hundred paces off,
You'll have to prove your skill. Now take your bow—   1885
You seem to keep it handy—and prepare

To shoot an apple from your own son's head.
But let me warn you, take your aim so well
You'll hit the apple on your first attempt,
1890 For if you miss, your head shall be the forfeit.

(*All give signs of horror.*)

TELL

But sir, what monstrous thing is this you ask?
You say I am to shoot at my own son—
No, no, my lord, you surely cannot mean that.
May God forbid! You could not seriously
1895 Demand this thing from any loving father.

GESSLER

You'll have to shoot the apple from his head.
This I demand, and I will see it done.

TELL

You say I am to take my bow and aim
At my own precious child? I'd rather die.

GESSLER

1900 Unless you shoot, the boy and you *both* die.

TELL

Am I to be the murderer of my child?
My lord, you have no children; you don't know
What stirs and throbs within a father's heart.

GESSLER

Now suddenly it seems you've grown discreet!

They told me that you were a dreamer, Tell, 1905
And that you shunned the ways of other men.
You love unusual things; so I selected
A special, daring deed just made for you.
Another man would think it over first,
But you will blindly tackle it, and boldly. 1910

BERTA

My lord, don't play with these poor people's lives.
You see them stand before you, pale and trembling,
So little are they used to jests from you.

GESSLER

Who says that I am jesting?

(*He grasps a branch that hangs overhead.*)

Here's the apple.
Make room there now, and let him take his distance 1915
As is the custom. I give him eighty steps,
No more, no less. He proudly made his boast
That he could hit his man at a hundred paces.
Now, archer, aim, and see that you don't miss.

RUDOLF DER HARRAS

My God, this has grown serious. Quickly, boy, 1920
Kneel down and beg the governor for your life.

WALTER FÜRST (*aside to* MELCHTAL, *who can hardly control his impatience*)

Control yourself. Keep calm, I beg of you!

BERTA (*to the* GOVERNOR)

That is enough, my lord. It is inhuman

To jest like this with any father's fears.
1925 And even if this man had forfeited
His life and limb to pay for his offense,
He must have suffered tenfold death by now.
Release him, then. Let him go home in peace.
He knows you now; he'll not forget this hour.
1930 He will remember, and his children's children.

GESSLER

Clear the way. Be quick! Why hesitate?
Your life is forfeited, and I can kill you;
But see, I mercifully place your fate
In your own skilled and highly practiced hand.
1935 You can't complain and call the sentence harsh
If you are made the master of your fate.
You boasted of your steady aim. All right!
Now, archer, is your chance to show your skill.
The mark is worthy and the prize is great.
1940 Another man can hit a bull's-eye too,
But I consider only him a master
Who trusts his skill in any situation,
Whose heart does not affect his eye and hand.

WALTER FÜRST (*prostrating himself before him*)

My lord, we recognize your sovereignty;
1945 But now let justice be replaced by mercy.
Take half of what I have, or take it all,
But spare this father such a dreadful deed.

WALTER TELL

Don't kneel before that wicked man, Grandfather.
Just tell me where to stand. I'm not afraid.
1950 My father even hits a bird in flight;

He will not miss his aim and hit his son.

STAUFFACHER

Are you not touched by this child's innocence?

RÖSSELMANN

Remember that there is a God in heaven
To whom you must account for all your deeds.

GESSLER (*pointing at the boy*)

Go, bind him to the linden tree.

WALTER TELL

                  Bind me?   1955
No, I will not be bound, I will hold still
Just like a lamb, and will not even breathe.
But if you bind me, then I can't be still;
I'll fight against my bonds until I'm free.

RUDOLF DER HARRAS

But you must let them blindfold you, my boy.   1960

WALTER TELL

Why blindfold me? Don't think I'll fear an arrow
From my own father's hand. I'll firmly stand
And wait for it, and never blink an eye.
Quick, Father, show how good a shot you are.
He doesn't know; he thinks he'll ruin us.   1965
To spite the tyrant, shoot, and hit your mark.

     (*He goes to the linden tree, and the apple is placed
              on his head.*)

MELCHTAL (*to the countrymen*)

What, shall this crime take place before our eyes?
Why did we swear the oath to stand together?

STAUFFACHER

It's all in vain because we have no weapons.
1970 Just see the pikes, as thick as trees around us.

MELCHTAL

If only we'd attacked them on the spot.
May God forgive the ones who urged delay.

GESSLER (*to* TELL)

Get at it now! You don't bear arms for nothing.
It's dangerous to bear a deadly weapon,
1975 And arrows may spring back upon the archer.
This right the peasants arrogantly claim
Offends the highest sovereign of the land.
Let none be armed except the overlord.
But if you people like to bear the bow,
1980 All right, then I'll provide you with a mark.

TELL (*bending the bow and fitting on an arrow*)

Clear the way! Make room!

STAUFFACHER

What, Tell? You mean to shoot! No! Never!
Your hands are trembling and your knees are shaking.

TELL (*lowering his crossbow*)

I'm feeling faint and dizzy.

WOMEN

God in heaven!

TELL (*to the* GOVERNOR)

Release me from this shot. Here is my heart.   1985

(*He tears his clothing from his breast.*)

Command your troopers now to strike me down.

GESSLER

I do not want your life, I want the shot.[10]
There's nothing you can't do; you're not afraid.
You're skilled with oars as well as with the bow;
You fear no storms when there's someone to save.   1990
Now, savior, save yourself; you save all others.

(TELL *stands in terrible inner struggle, with trembling
hands, turning his eyes alternately to the* GOVERNOR *and to
heaven. Suddenly he takes a second arrow from his quiver
and puts it in his doublet. The* GOVERNOR *notes all these
actions.*)

WALTER TELL (*under the linden tree*)

Shoot, Father, I am not afraid.

TELL

I must.

(*He controls himself and takes aim.*)

---

[10] Actually Gessler does not want the shot, as is seen in line 2034,
where he expresses extreme surprise. His purpose is to humiliate
Tell publicly.

RUDENZ (*who has been standing all the while, in a state
           of intense excitement barely restraining himself,
           now stepping forward*)

My lord, you will not force this matter further.
You'll *not* do that, for it was just a test.
1995 You have achieved your end. Severity,
When pushed too far, is sure to miss its aim,
Just as the bow will break when bent too far.

GESSLER

Keep silent till you're asked to speak!

RUDENZ

                                        I *will* speak!
I have a right to speak. The royal honor
2000 Is sacred, but a rule like yours breeds hate.
I know this isn't what the king intends.
My people don't deserve such cruelty,
And you have no authority for this.

GESSLER

You're growing bold, young man.

RUDENZ

                                  I've held my tongue
2005 Too long about the dreadful things I've seen.
I shut my eyes to what I knew went on;
My overflowing and rebellious heart
I kept subdued within my troubled breast.
But further silence would be treachery
2010 Against my country and against my king.

BERTA (*flinging herself between him and the*
  GOVERNOR)

Keep still; you'll only rouse his fury more.

RUDENZ

I turned against my people and renounced
My kinsmen, tore apart all bonds of nature
In order to attach myself to you.
I thought I furthered what was best for all   2015
When I helped fortify the kaiser's power.
But now the mist has cleared before my eyes,
And shuddering I see the precipice.
You have confused my independent judgment—
Deceived my honest heart. With best intentions   2020
I was about to wreck my land and people.

GESSLER

Insolent boy, such language to your lord?

RUDENZ

The emperor is my lord, not you. I'm free
As you by birth, and I can vie with you
In every knightly virtue and achievement.   2025
And if you did not represent the kaiser,
Whom I respect even when he is disgraced,
I'd throw the gauntlet down. You'd have to give
An answer by our knightly rule and custom.[11]
Yes! Beckon to your troopers now. I'm not   2030
Unarmed like them.

  (*He points at the people.*)

----

[11] Rudenz is talking about a challenge to a duel.

I have a sword, and who
Approaches me—

STAUFFACHER (*cries out*)

Look there! The apple's fallen!

(*While all have turned their attention to the side of the
stage where* BERTA *has thrown herself between* RUDENZ *and
the* GOVERNOR, TELL *has shot his arrow.*) [12]

RÖSSELMANN

The boy's alive!

MANY VOICES

The apple has been hit.

(WALTER FÜRST *staggers and is about to fall.* BERTA
supports him.)

GESSLER (*astonished*)

He shot the arrow? What? The man is crazy.

BERTA

2035 The boy's unharmed. Compose yourself, good father.

WALTER TELL (*comes running with the apple*)

The apple, Father, here's the apple. I knew it!
I knew you wouldn't miss and injure me.

---

[12] The skillful diversion of attention from Tell and Walter simpli-
fies the technical aspects of the shot. Moreover, on the stage, the
people can crowd around Walter so that he cannot be seen during
the shooting, and a pierced apple can be produced in place of the
other one.

(TELL *stands leaning forward, as if he wanted to follow the arrow. His crossbow drops from his hand. When he sees the boy coming, he hurries to meet him with open arms, lifts him up, and presses him fervently to his heart. From this position he falls down exhausted. All the people remain still, deeply moved.*)

BERTA

Oh, gracious God in heaven!

WALTER FÜRST (*to father and son*)

Children, my children!

STAUFFACHER

God be praised!

LEUTHOLD

I say, that was some shot!
They'll speak of it forever and a day.   2040

RUDOLF DER HARRAS

They will be talking of this archer Tell
As long as mountains stand on their foundations.

(*He hands the apple to the* GOVERNOR.)

GESSLER

By heaven! The apple pierced right through the center!
That was a master shot. I have to praise it.

RÖSSELMANN

The shot was good, that's true, but woe to him   2045
Whose malice drove this man to tempting God.

STAUFFACHER

Come to your senses, Tell. You have redeemed
Yourself, and you are free to go back home.

RÖSSELMANN

Come, take the boy back to his mother now.

(*They start to take him away.*)

GESSLER

2050 One moment, Tell!

TELL (*coming back*)

What is it, sir?

GESSLER

You put
A second arrow in your doublet. Oh yes,
I noticed that. What was the arrow for?

TELL (*embarrassed*)

It's just a custom, sir, among us hunters.

GESSLER

No, Tell, I cannot let that answer pass.
2055 I think there must have been some other reason.
Don't hesitate. Just speak the candid truth;
No matter what, I'll guarantee your life.
Say, why the second arrow?

TELL

All right then, sir,

Because you've promised not to take my life,
I'll tell you all the truth, straight from my heart. 2060

(*He draws the arrow from his doublet and looks at
the* GOVERNOR *with a frightful gaze.*)

This second arrow would have pierced through *you*
If I had hit my own beloved child.
And you, yes, truly—I could not have missed.

GESSLER

All right then, Tell! I guaranteed your life.
I gave my knightly word, and I will keep it. 2065
But since I recognize your evil thoughts,
I'll have you taken off and put in prison
Where neither moon nor sun will shine on you,
So that I may be safe from flying arrows.
Arrest him, men, and bind his hands. 2070

(*They bind him.*)

STAUFFACHER

What, sir!
You dare to treat like this a man on whom
God's hand has been so visibly revealed?

GESSLER

Let's see if it will rescue him again.
Now take him to my boat; I'll follow you.
I'll carry him myself to Küssnacht castle. 2075

RÖSSELMANN

You can't do that, nor can the emperor.
That violates the freedom in our charters.

GESSLER

Where are they? Has the emperor confirmed them?
Indeed he hasn't. This favor you must first
2080 Deserve by your complete obedience.
You're rebels all against the kaiser's power,
And secretly you're plotting insurrection.
I know you men. I see through all of you.
This time I'm taking only one away,
2085 But you are all involved and share his guilt.
Learn to obey in silence, if you're clever.

(*He leaves.* BERTA, RUDENZ, HARRAS, *and the troopers
follow.* FRIESSHARD *and* LEUTHOLD *stay behind.*)

WALTER FÜRST (*in violent anguish*)

Now it is done. He has resolved to bring
Destruction down on me and all my house.

STAUFFACHER (*to* TELL)

Why did you have to irritate the tyrant?

TELL

2090 Let those who felt my pain control themselves.

STAUFFACHER

Now all is over; everything is lost.
We too are chained and bound along with you.

COUNTRYMEN (*surrounding* TELL)

With you, our hope, our last resort is gone.

LEUTHOLD (*approaching him*)

I'm sorry, Tell, I must obey the order.

TELL

Farewell!

WALTER TELL (*clinging to him in great anguish*)
    Oh Father, Father, my dear father! 2095

TELL (*raising his arms toward heaven*)
Up yonder is your Father. Call on him.

STAUFFACHER

Can I take any message to your wife?

TELL (*pressing the boy fervently to his breast*)
The boy's unhurt, and God will help me too.

    (*He tears himself away abruptly and follows the
    guards.*)

ACT FOUR

SCENE I

The east shore of Lake Lucerne.[1]

(Steep and strangely shaped cliffs close the prospect to the west. The lake is agitated; there is violent roaring and rushing of wind, accompanied by lightning and thunder.)

*(*KUNZ VON GERSAU, *the* FISHERMAN, *and the* FISHERMAN'S SON *are talking.)* [2]

KUNZ

I saw it all. With my own eyes I saw it.
2100 It happened as I've said; you can believe me.

FISHERMAN

Our Tell a prisoner on his way to Küssnacht—
Our country's bravest man, its strongest arm
If ever there should be a fight for freedom.

KUNZ

The governor himself is taking him
2105 By boat. They were about to go on board

---

[1] There are various indications that the locale is near Sisikon.
[2] The Fisherman, not named, is Ruodi, and he addresses the boy by the name "Jenni," as in Act I, scene 1. The name was deleted in the translation for reasons of meter and rhyme.

132

As I myself was putting out from Flüelen.
But then this storm that's breaking over us,
Which made me put to shore so hurriedly,
May well have hindered them in their departure.

FISHERMAN

Tell is in chains and in the viceroy's power!   2110
Believe me, he will be entombed so deep
He'll never see the light of day again,
For Gessler surely fears the just revenge
Of someone he has wronged and angered so.

KUNZ

They say the noble Lord von Attinghausen,   2115
Our former magistrate, is near his death.

FISHERMAN

We've lost the final anchor of our hope.
He was the only one who still spoke out,
Defending justice and the people's rights.

KUNZ

The storm is getting worse. I must be off.   2120
I'll stop and seek my shelter in the village,
For it's impossible to leave today.

(*Exit.*)

FISHERMAN

Our Tell a prisoner, and the baron dead!
Now, tyranny, raise up your haughty brow.
Cast shame aside! The voice of truth is stilled;   2125

The eyes that saw the right are blinded now;
The arms that were to save us are in chains.

FISHERMAN'S SON

It's hailing, Father. Come into the house.
You shouldn't be outside in such a storm.

FISHERMAN

2130 Blow, winds! You lightning bolts, flash down your fire! [3]
And burst, you clouds! Pour waterfalls and streams
From heaven, drown the land in floods! Destroy
The germ of generations yet unborn!
You raging elements, be masters here!
2135 Return, wild beasts, you bears and wolves, return!
To you belongs the land, the wilderness.
Who wants to live here now without his freedom?

FISHERMAN'S SON

The wind is raging on the cliff. Just listen!
There never was such roaring in this gorge.

FISHERMAN

2140 To aim directly at his own child's head—
Such things were never asked of any father.
No wonder then that nature should rebel
In savage wrath. And it would not surprise me
If all these cliffs should plunge into the lake,
2145 If all these mighty peaks and towers of ice
That since creation day have never melted
Should thaw and topple from their lofty crests,

---

[3] In this passage Schiller was influenced by the famous storm
speech in Shakespeare's *King Lear,* Act III, scene 2.

If mountains should crash down, the ancient crags
Collapse, a second Deluge swallow up
The habitations of all living men.   2150

(*The ringing of bells is heard.*)

FISHERMAN'S SON

The bells are ringing on the mountain. Listen!
Somebody must have seen a boat in danger,
And rings the bells that we may pray for it.

(*He ascends a knoll.*)

FISHERMAN

I pity any boat that's caught out there
To rock and sway in such a fearful cradle.   2155
The helmsman and his helm are useless then;
The storm is master. Man is tossed about
Just like a ball by wind and waves. No bay
Can offer him protection near or far.
Inhospitable cliffs rise steeply up;   2160
They stare at him, without a ledge to grasp,
And show him only steep and stony breasts.

FISHERMAN'S SON (*pointing to the left*)

Father, a boat! It's coming down from Flüelen.

FISHERMAN

May God have mercy on those wretched men!
When storms become entangled in these gorges,   2165
They roar and rage like captive beasts of prey
And fling themselves against the iron bars.
Howling, they try to find escape in vain,

For all around the cliffs imprison them
2170   And wall them up inside the narrow pass.

(*He climbs up on the knoll.*)

FISHERMAN'S SON

It is the viceroy's boat from Uri, Father.
I recognize its red deck and its flag.

FISHERMAN

By God's eternal judgment! That's his boat.
The governor himself is sailing there
2175   And has on board the burden of his crime.
How quickly the avenger's arm has reached him!
Now he must feel a stronger lord than he.
The wind and waves will not obey his voice;
These cliffs will not bend down or bow their heads
2180   Before his hat. Oh no, my son, don't pray.
Don't stay the arm of judgment with your prayers.

FISHERMAN'S SON

Oh, I don't pray to save the governor.
I pray for Tell, who's also on the boat.

FISHERMAN

Oh, folly of the sightless elements—
2185   Must you, to strike the only one who's guilty,
Destroy the boat together with the boatmen?

FISHERMAN'S SON

Look, they had safely passed the Buggisgrat,
But now the power of the storm rebounding

Upon them from the mighty Teufelsmünster
Is hurling them against the Axenberg.[4]   2190
I cannot see them any more.

FISHERMAN

                                    There stands
Hackmesser cliff that's broken many a boat.
If they do not steer wisely past those rocks,
Their boat will dash to pieces on the crag
That slopes down sharply to the water's edge.   2195
But they've on board a good and practiced steersman;
If anyone can save them, Tell's the man.
But surely they have chained his arms and hands.

(WILHELM TELL *enters, with his crossbow. He comes in
rapidly, looks around in surprise, and shows the most violent agitation. When he reaches the center of the stage he
falls upon his knees, stretching out his hands first toward
the earth, then toward heaven.*)

FISHERMAN'S SON (*observing him*)

Look, Father, who's the man that's kneeling there?

FISHERMAN

He's clutching at the earth with both his hands.   2200
He looks as if he were beside himself.

FISHERMAN'S SON (*coming closer*)

What's this I see? Come, Father, come and look!

---

4 The Buggisgrat and Hackmesser (line 2192) are steep cliffs of the
Axenberg or Axen Mountain; the Teufelsmünster is a steep rock on
the opposite shore.

FISHERMAN (*approaching*)

Who is it? God in heaven, is it Tell?
How did you get here? Speak!

FISHERMAN'S SON

                                   Weren't you just now
2205 A prisoner on that boat, and bound in chains?

FISHERMAN

And weren't they taking you across to Küssnacht?

TELL (*getting up*)

I have escaped.

FISHERMAN *and* BOY

                    Escaped! A miracle!

FISHERMAN'S SON

Where did you come from?

TELL

                              From the boat there.

FISHERMAN

                                             What?

FISHERMAN'S SON (*at the same time*)

Where is the viceroy?

TELL

                    Tossing on the waves.

FISHERMAN

How is it possible that you escaped 2210
Both from your bonds and from the stormy sea?

TELL

Through God's almighty providence. Now hear me.

FISHERMAN *and* BOY

Yes, tell us everything!

TELL

You heard what happened
Today in Altdorf?

FISHERMAN

Yes, I know it all.

TELL

The viceroy captured me and had me bound. 2215
He planned to take me on to Küssnacht castle.

FISHERMAN

And that he then embarked with you at Flüelen—
We know all that. But how did you escape?

TELL

I lay on deck, securely tied with ropes,
Defenseless and resigned. I had no hope 2220
Of looking at the shining sun again
Or on the faces of my wife and children,
And with despair I viewed the watery waste.

FISHERMAN

Unhappy man.

TELL

                          And so we moved along,
2225 The governor and Rudolf and their men.
      My quiver and my crossbow lay astern,
      Right at the helm, beside the steersman's place—
      And just as we had reached the Axenberg,
      Below the Lesser Axen, God decreed
2230 That suddenly a dreadful storm break out
      And beat upon us from St. Gotthard's gorge,
      So that our oarsmen all lost heart and hope
      And thought we faced a miserable drowning.
      Then one attendant of the governor
2235 Approached him, and I heard him speak these words:
      "You see your danger and ours too, my lord,
      And that we hover on the brink of death.
      Our oarsmen are confused from growing fear
      And don't know what to do, for they're not used
2240 To steering in the storm. But there is Tell,
      A mighty man who steers a boat with skill.
      What if we were to use him in our danger?"
      Then spoke the viceroy: "Tell, if you could help,
      And felt that you could save us from this storm,
2245 I might consent to free you from your bonds."
      I answered, "Yes, my lord, with help from God
      I feel that I could get us out of this."
      So I was freed from bonds and took my place
      Beside the helm and steered a steady course.
2250 But from the corner of my eye I saw
      My weapon lying near, and watched the shore
      For any spot where I might leap to freedom.

And when I saw a flat and rocky crag
That jutted like a ledge into the lake— [5]

FISHERMAN

I know it well. It's at the Greater Axen,   2255
But I should think it's much too high and steep
To reach by leaping out of any boat.

TELL

I shouted to the men to row with force
Till we could reach and pass the rocky ledge.
The worst would be behind us there, I cried.   2260
And as we came upon it, rowing stoutly,
I prayed to God for mercy, braced myself,
And pressed with all my strength to force the stern
To shore and toward the rocky precipice.
Then quickly I snatched up my near-by weapon   2265
And leaped upon the rocky ledge above.
And as I jumped I gave a mighty shove,
To thrust the boat adrift upon the lake.
There let it ride the waves as God decrees.
Thus I am freed from violence of storms   2270
And from the greater violence of men.

FISHERMAN

The Lord has truly wrought a miracle
For you! I scarcely can believe my eyes.
But tell me, where do you intend to go?

---

[5] The ledge is now called "Tells Platte." Here a small chapel now
stands, with frescoes depicting scenes from the play. See also lines
2259 and 2266 and the illustration following p. xvi.

2275   There can be no security for you
If Gessler should escape this storm alive.

TELL

I heard him say, when I still lay aboard
In bonds, that he would put to shore at Brunnen
And take me to his fort by way of Schwyz.

FISHERMAN

2280   You think that he will make the trip by land?

TELL

That's what he plans.

FISHERMAN

                   Then you must hide at once.
Don't count on God to save you from him twice.

TELL

Which is the shortest way to Arth and Küssnacht?

FISHERMAN

The public road goes there by way of Steinen,
2285   But there's a shorter and more secret path
My son can guide you on, by way of Lowerz.

TELL (*shaking his hand*)

May God reward you for your kindness. Good-by.

(*As he is leaving, he turns back.*)

Did not you also take the Rütli oath?
I think I heard them mention you.

FISHERMAN

                          I did.
I was with them and took the oath of union.   2290

TELL

Then do a favor for me. Go to Bürglen
Quickly and find my wife, who's in despair.
Tell her that I escaped and that I'm safe.

FISHERMAN

But shall I tell her where you've gone to hide?

TELL

You'll find her father there at home with her,   2295
And others, too, who took the Rütli oath.
Tell them they must be brave and resolute,
For I am free and master of my strength,
And soon they will hear further news from me.

FISHERMAN

What do you have in mind? Come, won't you tell?   2300

TELL

You'll hear about it after I am through.

      (*Exit.*)

FISHERMAN

Show him the way. May God protect him well.
Whatever he has planned, he'll surely do.

      (*Exeunt.*)

Scene II

The baronial castle of Attinghausen.

(*The* Baron *is in an armchair, dying.* Walter Fürst, Stauffacher, Melchtal, *and* Baumgarten *are busy around him.* Walter Tell *is kneeling before the dying man.*)

Walter Fürst

It's over with him now. He's passed away.

Stauffacher

2305 He isn't lying like a dead man. Look,
The feather at his lips is moving still.
His sleep is calm; his features smile in peace.

(Baumgarten *goes to the door and speaks with someone.*)

Walter Fürst (*to* Baumgarten)

Who's at the door?

Baumgarten (*coming back*)

Your daughter, Hedwig Tell.
She wants to speak with you and see the boy.

(Walter Tell *gets up.*)

Walter Fürst

2310 How can I comfort her when *I* need comfort?
Is every sorrow heaped upon my head?

HEDWIG (*forcing her way in*)

Where is my child? You have to let me see him.

STAUFFACHER

Be calm. Remember death is in this house.

HEDWIG (*running to the boy*)

My little Walter! You are safe!

WALTER TELL (*clinging to her*)

Poor Mother!

HEDWIG

It's really true? You're sure you are not hurt?   2315

(*She gazes at him with anxious solicitude.*)

And is it possible? He aimed at you?
How could he do it? Oh, he has no heart!
How could he shoot an arrow at his child?

WALTER FÜRST

It was in grief and anguish that he acted.
He was compelled; their lives were in the balance.   2320

HEDWIG

Oh, if he had a father's heart within him,
He would have sooner died a thousand deaths.

STAUFFACHER

You should be grateful for God's providence
That guided things so well—

HEDWIG

                                        Can I forget
2325 What could have happened? God in heaven; If I
Should live a hundred years,[6] I'd always see
My boy stand bound, his father aiming at him,
And always would the arrow pierce my heart.

MELCHTAL

If you knew how the viceroy taunted him!

HEDWIG

2330 The cruel hearts of men! Offend their pride,
And nothing matters to them any more.
In furious contest they will blindly risk
Their children's heads and break a mother's heart.

BAUMGARTEN

Is not your husband's fate severe enough
2335 Without your wounding him with your reproach?
Have you no feeling left for his ordeal?

HEDWIG (*turning and staring at him*)

And you? Have you but tears for his misfortune?
And where were all of you when they put bonds
On this good man? How did you help him then?
2340 You just looked on, and let the horror happen.
You made no protest when they dragged your friend
Right from your midst. Is that how he, how Tell
Has treated you? Did he just stand there too,

---

[6] The German reads "eighty years," a general expression like the English "hundred years."

And only sympathize when in pursuit
The troopers threatened, and the angry lake   2345
Surged up before you? He didn't show his pity
With idle tears. Forgetting wife and children,
He leaped into the boat and rescued you.

WALTER FÜRST

How could we try to rescue him by force?
For that we were too few, and none was armed.   2350

HEDWIG (*flinging herself upon his breast*)

You too have lost him, Father, and you'll miss him.
Our country, all of us, have lost him now.
We'll miss him sorely, and he'll miss us too.
May God deliver him from cold despair!
No friend's consoling words will penetrate   2355
That lonely dungeon. If he fell sick in there!
Yes, in the damp and darkness of that prison
He will be sick. Just as the Alpine rose
Must fade and die in low and swampy air,
There is no life for him but in the light,   2360
In sunlight and in gentle mountain air.
Imprisoned! He! His breath of life is freedom.
He cannot breathe the prison air and live.

STAUFFACHER

Now calm yourself. We all will act together
To break the prison doors and set him free.   2365

HEDWIG

What can you do without his help, you men?
As long as Tell was free, there still was hope;
Then innocence still had a champion,

And persecuted people had a helper.
2370 Tell could have saved you all, but all of you
Together cannot free him from his chains.

(*The* BARON *wakes up*.)

BAUMGARTEN

He's moving. Quiet.

ATTINGHAUSEN (*raising himself up*)

Where is he?

STAUFFACHER

Who?

ATTINGHAUSEN

I miss him.
He has deserted me in my last moments.

STAUFFACHER

He means his nephew. Have they sent for him?

WALTER FÜRST

2375 They sent for him, my lord. Be comforted.
He found his heart at last and he is ours.

ATTINGHAUSEN

And has he spoken for his fatherland?

STAUFFACHER

With heroism.

ATTINGHAUSEN

But why is he not here
To take my final blessing? I can feel
The end come on; my life will soon be over. 2380

STAUFFACHER

No, my good lord, don't talk that way. Your sleep
Has much refreshed you, and your eyes are clear.

ATTINGHAUSEN

All pain is life, yet that has left me too.
My suffering is gone, as is my hope.

(*He notices* WALTER TELL.)

Who is the boy?

WALTER FÜRST

Please bless him, noble sir. 2385
He is my grandson, and he's fatherless.

(HEDWIG *kneels down with the boy before the dying man.*)

ATTINGHAUSEN

And fatherless I leave you all behind.
What wretched fate, that in these final moments
My eyes have seen the ruin of my country.
To think that I have reached this ripe old age 2390
To see my every hope depart with me.

STAUFFACHER (*to* WALTER FÜRST)

How can we let him die in hopeless grief?

Why can't we ease his final hour of life
By giving him a ray of hope? My lord,
2395 Lift up your spirits; we are not forsaken.
We are not lost beyond deliverance.

ATTINGHAUSEN

Who will deliver you?

WALTER FÜRST

We will, ourselves.
We men in these three cantons pledged our word
That we will drive the tyrants from the land.
2400 We formed a union, and a sacred oath
Unites us all. Before the present year
Has run its course, we'll take concerted action.
Your dust will lie at rest in a free land.

ATTINGHAUSEN

It's really so? The union has been formed?

MELCHTAL

2405 Yes, all three forest cantons will rise up
On the appointed day. Our plans are all
In readiness; the secret's closely kept
Until this hour, though hundreds share its knowledge.
The ground beneath the tyrant's feet is hollow.
2410 The days of this regime are numbered. Soon
There'll be no trace remaining of their rule.

ATTINGHAUSEN

But what about their strongholds on our soil?

MELCHTAL

They all will fall on the appointed day.

ATTINGHAUSEN

And do the nobles share in this new union?

STAUFFACHER

We count on their assistance, should we need it.   2415
As yet none but the countrymen have sworn.

ATTINGHAUSEN (*raising himself up in great astonishment*)

If countrymen have dared so bold a deed
All by themselves, without the aid of nobles,
Relied so much on their own strength and means,
Good—then we nobles are no longer needed,   2420
And we can meet our death with confidence
That life goes on, that mankind's glory will
Hereafter be maintained by other hands.

(*He lays his hand upon the head of the child who is kneeling before him.*)

From this child's head, on which the apple lay,
Shall spring your new and better liberty.   2425
The old is falling down, and times are changing;
A better life is rising from the ruins.

STAUFFACHER (*to* WALTER FÜRST)

Look what a light is shining in his eyes!
That's not the fading of the flame of life;
It is the radiance of new life and hope.   2430

ATTINGHAUSEN

The nobles are descending from their castles
And swearing their allegiance to the cities.
In Üchtland and in Thurgau it has started,
And noble Bern lifts up her sovereign head,
2435   And Freiburg is a fortress of the free,
While busy Zurich calls her guilds to arms
To form a warlike army. The power of kings
Is broken on their everlasting walls.

(*He speaks the following lines in a prophetic tone,
his voice rising in enthusiasm.*)

I see the ruling princes and the knights
2440   Come riding up, all clad in steel and armor,
To wage a cruel war on harmless herdsmen.
There'll be a fight for life and death, and fame
Will come to many a pass in bloody combat.
A peasant will advance with naked breast
2445   And willingly confront a host of lances;
He'll shatter them, and knighthood's flower will fall
And freedom's flag be raised in victory.

(*He grasps* WALTER FÜRST'S *and* STAUFFACHER'S
hands.)

Hold fast together then, forever fast.
Let no free canton stand apart from others.
2450   Set beacon lights and watches on your mountains
So that your members may assemble quickly.
United, be united . . . united. . . .

(*He falls back upon his pillow. His lifeless hands continue to grasp the others'.* FÜRST *and* STAUFFACHER *look at
him for some moments in silence. Then they step aside,*

each given over to his sorrow. Meanwhile the vassals have quietly come in. They approach, some showing calm, others violent grief. Some kneel down by his side and weep over his hand. During the wordless scene the castle bells are rung.)

RUDENZ (*entering hurriedly and joining the others*)

Is he alive? Can he still hear me speak?

WALTER FÜRST (*with his face turned aside, gesturing toward the dead man*)

You are our liege lord and protector, sir,
And now this castle bears another name.   2455

RUDENZ (*gazing at the body with deep emotion*)

Oh God! Does my repentance come too late?
Why couldn't he have lived a moment longer
To see the change within my heart?
I once disdained his true and prudent voice
When he yet moved in light upon the earth.   2460
Now he is gone forever, and he leaves
A heavy debt that I must pay for him.
But tell me, did he die still angry with me?

STAUFFACHER

Before he died, he heard what you had done
And praised and blessed the courage of your speech.   2465

RUDENZ (*kneeling by the dead man*)

Yes, hallowed body of a worthy man,
You lifeless corpse, upon your death-cold hand
I take an oath that I have torn away
All foreign bonds and freed myself forever.

2470 I have been given back to my own people.
I am a Swiss and always will be one
With all my heart and soul—

(*He rises.*)

Mourn for our friend,
Our common father, yet do not despair.
It's not his wealth alone that I inherit;
2475 I feel his heart, his spirit, rise in me,
And in the vigor of my youth I'll do
The tasks he left unfinished in old age.
Give me your hand, you venerable father.[7]
And give me yours. You too, Melchtal, your hand.
2480 Don't hesitate or turn away from me.
Receive my oath, accept my loyal pledge.

WALTER FÜRST

Give him your hands. The heart that has returned
Deserves our trust.

MELCHTAL

You once despised the peasant.
How can we look to you and trust you now?

RUDENZ

2485 Don't hold in mind the errors of my youth.

STAUFFACHER (*to* MELCHTAL)

"Be united!" Those were our father's words.
Let us remember that.

---

[7] Walter Fürst.

MELCHTAL

Here is my hand.
A peasant's handclasp is a true man's word,
My noble sir. What is the knight without us?
The peasant's rank is older, too, than yours.   2490

RUDENZ

I give it honor, and my sword shall guard it.

MELCHTAL

My lord, the arm that clears and cultivates
The stubborn soil to make it more productive
Can also shield the human breast.

RUDENZ

Then you
Shall be the shield for me, and I for you;   2495
So shall we each grow stronger through the other.
But why this talking, when our fatherland
Is still a prey to foreign tyranny?
When we have swept away our enemy,
We'll reconcile our differences in peace.   2500

(After pausing a moment)

You do not speak? You have no word for me?
What, do I still deserve distrust from you?
Then I am forced to go against your wishes
And pry into the secrets of your union.
You met and took your oath on Rütli meadow.   2505
I know it all; I know what was agreed.
And though you would not let me share your secret,
I've guarded it just like a sacred trust.

I never was my country's enemy,
2510 And never would I have opposed your cause.
But it was wrong to put off your revolt.
The hour is pressing; we must act at once.
Already Tell's a victim of delay.

STAUFFACHER

We swore that we would wait till Christmas time.

RUDENZ

2515 I wasn't there. I did not take the oath.
Wait if you must, but I will act.

MELCHTAL

You would—?

RUDENZ

I count myself among my country's leaders,
And my first duty now is to protect you.

WALTER FÜRST

Your first and your most sacred duty is
2520 To lay these dear remains into the grave.

RUDENZ

When we have set our country free, we'll place
Our new-won victory wreath upon his bier.
Dear friends, it's not your cause alone that moves me;
I have my own to settle in this fight
2525 Against the tyrant. Hear me now, and know
My Berta's disappeared; they dragged her off
From us by secret means, with shameless boldness.

STAUFFACHER

You say the tyrant dared such violence
Against a lady, free and born a noble?

RUDENZ

Dear friends, I gladly promised you assistance,   2530
And now I come imploring help from you.
The one I love was stolen, dragged away,
And who knows where that madman's hiding her,
Or with what crime and outrage they make bold
To force her heart to some detested marriage.   2535
Do not forsake me; help me rescue her.
She loves you, and deserves from her own land
That all should take up arms in her behalf.

WALTER FÜRST

What course do you propose?

RUDENZ

                  I do not know.
In this dark mystery that hides her fate,   2540
In this anxiety of monstrous doubts
When I cannot lay hold of certainty,
One thing is clear as daylight in my mind:
We'll free her only if we rescue her
Out of the ruins of the tyrant's power.   2545
We'll have to take the castles, one and all,
And press into her dungeon when they fall.

MELCHTAL

Come, lead us on! We'll follow. Why put off
Until tomorrow what we can do today?
When we assembled on the Rütli, Tell   2550

Was free. The monstrous thing had not yet happened.
But time brings other laws and other measures.
Who is the coward that is still afraid?

RUDENZ (*to* STAUFFACHER *and* WALTER FÜRST)

Meanwhile take up your arms, prepared to strike,
2555 And wait for fiery signals on the mountains;
For faster than a boat can bring dispatches,
The message of our victory shall reach you.
And when you see the welcome light of flames,
Then strike our foe with lightning speed and thunder,
2560 And break the house of tyranny asunder.

(*All leave.*)

SCENE III

The Hohle Gasse, *a deep and narrow road near Küss-nacht.*[8]

(*The road slopes down steeply from the back between rocks, and wayfarers are seen on the high point before they appear on the stage. Rocks and cliffs enclose the entire scene. On one of the ridges closest to the front is a ledge overgrown with brushwood.*)

TELL (*entering with his crossbow*)

He has to go along this narrow road.
There is no other way that leads to Küssnacht.

---

[8] Küssnacht is on the northern end of Lake Lucerne. It is now in Canton Lucerne, but at the time of the events of the play it was in Schwyz, one of the two cantons (Schwyz and Uri) over which Gessler ruled.

I'll do it here; the place is favorable.
The elderbush will hide me over there,
And from that point my arrow's flight can reach him.   2565
The narrow road will hinder the pursuers.
Now, viceroy, settle your account with heaven.
You have to go, for time's run out on you.

I led a harmless, quiet hunter's life.
My bow was bent for woodland game alone,   2570
My mind was free from any thoughts of murder.
You frightened me away from peaceful ways;
You changed the natural milk of human kindness
To rankling, bitter poison in my breast.
You have accustomed me to monstrous things.   2575
A man who had to aim at his own child
Can surely hit his adversary's heart.

I must protect my faithful wife, my children,
Against your awful anger, Governor.
When I was forced as punishment to draw   2580
The bow and level it with trembling hands,
When you with such infernal glee compelled me
To take my aim at my beloved child,
When I was pleading helplessly before you—
I vowed then, deep within my heart and soul,   2585
A dreadful oath that only God could hear,
That I would aim my bow and arrow next
Straight at your heart. The promise that I made
Amid the hellish torments of this day
Is now a sacred debt which I will pay.   2590

You are my lord, my kaiser's governor;
But even he, the king, would not have dared
What have you done. He sent you to this country
To deal out justice sternly, for he's angry,
But not with fiendish pleasure to make bold   2595

To do such wrong unpunished, uncontrolled.
There is a God to punish and avenge.

Come now, you messenger of bitter pain,
My dearest jewel and my greatest treasure.
2600 I'll set a mark for you that until now
No fervent plea could ever penetrate,
But you shall pierce it irresistibly.
And you, my trusted bowstring, you so often
Have served me faithfully in joyous sport;
2605 Do not desert me in this dreadful hour.
Hold fast this one more time, my faithful string,
Who often sped my bitter arrow's flight.
If it should feebly from my fingers fly,
I have no second one with which to try.

(*Wayfarers pass across the stage.*)

2610 I'll sit down here upon this bench of stone
Constructed for the travelers' rest and comfort,
For there's no home out here. Each wanderer
Goes past the others quickly and estranged,
And doesn't ask about their pains and cares.
2615 The worried, anxious merchant passes by;
The pious monk, the lightly-laden pilgrim,
The sullen thief and then the jolly minstrel,
The pack-horse driver, with his burdened beast,
Who hails from distant lands—they come and go,
2620 For every road leads somewhere at the last.
Each has his business; each goes on his way.
My way and business are to kill today.

(*He sits down.*)

There was a time when you rejoiced, dear children,
At Father's safe return from hunting trips,
2625 For when he came, he always brought a gift.

Sometimes it was a pretty Alpine flower,
Sometimes a curious bird or ammonite
Such as the travelers find upon the mountains.
But now he's on the hunt for other game;
He sits beside this road with thoughts of murder   2630
And waits to kill his enemy from ambush.
But still he thinks of you alone, dear children,
And only to protect your innocence
Against the vengeance of a mighty foe,
He will take aim to kill, and draw his bow.   2635

    (*He rises.*)

I lie in wait for noble game. The hunter
Will never weary when he roams about
For days in winter's bitter cold and frost.
He risks his life in leaps from rock to rock,
And climbs the steep and slippery mountainsides   2640
And clings to them, glued on with his own blood,
So he can hunt a paltry chamois down.
But now I seek a far more precious prize:
My mortal enemy, who seeks my ruin.

    (*In the distance is heard lively music, coming closer.*)

Throughout my life I've always used the bow;   2645
I've trained and practiced by the rules of archers.
I often hit the bull's-eye of the target
And won a pretty prize to carry home
From matches. But today I want to make
My master-shot and win the greatest prize   2650
In all the broad expanses of these mountains.

    (*A bridal party passes across the stage and goes up the
narrow road.* TELL *watches it pass, leaning on his bow.*
STÜSSI, *the ranger, joins him.*)

STÜSSI

That is the overseer of Mörlischachen [9]
And that's his wedding party. He is rich
And owns ten herds of cattle in the Alps.
2655   He's taking home his bride from Immensee.
And there will be a feast tonight at Küssnacht.
Come with us. Every honest man's invited.

TELL

A gloomy guest is not for wedding feasts.

STÜSSI

If worry weighs you down, throw it aside.
2660   Accept what comes your way; the times are hard,
So make the most of pleasure when it comes.
Here is a feast and elsewhere burial.

TELL

And often one comes right behind the other.

STÜSSI

So goes the world; misfortune everywhere.
2665   In Canton Glarus there has been a landslide;
One side of Glärnisch peak has fallen down.

TELL

Are even mountains tottering and falling?
There's not a thing on earth that's standing firm.

---

[9] A monastery.

STÜSSI

One hears of strange things happening everywhere.
I spoke, for instance, with a man from Baden;   2670
He said a knight was on his way to court,
And on the way, a swarm of hornets came
And settled on his horse, attacking it
With painful stings until it fell down dead.
So he went on and came to court on foot.   2675

TELL

The weak are also furnished with a sting.

(ARMGARD *enters with several children and takes her
position at the entrance of the narrow pass.*)

STÜSSI

They say it means disaster for our land—
Unnatural and dreadful happenings.

TELL

Such things are happening each day somewhere;
No supernatural acts need make them known.   2680

STÜSSI

Well, lucky he who tills his field in peace
And sits at home among his own, untroubled.

TELL

The most devout cannot abide in peace
If it's displeasing to his evil neighbor.

(TELL *often looks with restless expectation toward the high point of the road.*)

STÜSSI

2685   Good-by. Are you expecting someone here?

TELL

I am.

STÜSSI

A happy homeward journey then.
You are from Uri? Our viceroy was up there,
And we're expecting his return today.

A TRAVELER (*entering*)

Do not expect the governor today.
2690   The streams are flooded from the heavy rains,
And all the bridges have been washed away.

(TELL *rises.*)

ARMGARD (*coming forward*)

He will not come.

STÜSSI

You want to ask for something?

ARMGARD

Indeed I do.

STÜSSI

> But why then stand around
> In narrow roads where you obstruct his way?

ARMGARD

He can't escape me here. He has to listen.   2695

FRIESSHARD (*coming down the narrow road hastily, calling toward the stage*)

Make way! My gracious lord, the governor,
Is close behind me, riding down the pass.

(TELL *leaves.*)

ARMGARD (*excitedly*)

The governor is coming.

(*She goes toward the front of the stage with her children.* GESSLER *and* RUDOLF DER HARRAS *appear on horseback at the high point of the road.*)

STÜSSI (*to* FRIESSHARD)

> How could you cross
> The stream when every bridge is swept away?

FRIESSHARD

We fought a battle with the lake, my friend;   2700
So now we're not afraid of Alpine streams.

STÜSSI

You were afloat in that terrific storm?

FRIESSHARD

We were. I will remember that forever.

STÜSSI

Do stay and tell me!

FRIESSHARD

           I can't. I must go on
2705 And tell them that the governor is coming.

(*He leaves.*)

STÜSSI

If decent folk had been aboard that ship,
It surely would have sunk with all on board,
But men like these are safe from fire and water.

(*He looks around.*)

Where is that hunter I was talking to?

(*Exit.*)

(GESSLER *and* RUDOLF DER HARRAS *enter on horse-back.*)

GESSLER

2710 Say what you will, I am the kaiser's servant
And must consider how to please him best.
He didn't send me here to flatter people
And deal too gently with them. He expects
Obedience. The question here is whether
2715 The peasant or the kaiser will be master.

ARMGARD

Now is the moment. Now I'll make my plea.

(She approaches fearfully.)

GESSLER

I didn't hang the hat for fun in Altdorf,
Nor even as a test of people's hearts.
I know them all too well. I put it up
That they might learn to bend their stubborn necks   2720
Which now they carry proudly and erect.
I placed this inconvenient device,
Exactly in their way, where they must pass,
So that they have to see it there and be
Reminded of their lord, whom they forget.   2725

RUDOLF

But sir, the people also have some rights.

GESSLER

It's not the time to weigh and settle those.
Great matters are in progress. The royal house
Desires to grow, and what the father started
So gloriously, his noble son will finish.[10]   2730
This country is a stone upon our path.
One way or other, these cantons must submit.

(They start to pass on, but ARMGARD *throws herself down before the* GOVERNOR.*)*

---

[10] Rudolf of Hapsburg (reigned 1273–1291) and his son Albrecht (reigned 1298–1308).

ARMGARD

Have mercy, Governor! My lord, have mercy!

GESSLER

Why block my passage on this public road?
2735　Get back, I say!

ARMGARD

　　　　　　　　My husband lies in prison;
These hungry orphans cry for bread. My lord,
Have pity on our terrible distress!

RUDOLF

Who are you anyway? And who's your husband?

ARMGARD

A gatherer of hay from Rigi Mountain
2740　Who mows the wild free grass above the chasm,
Along the steep and rugged precipice
Where even cattle do not dare to climb—

RUDOLF (*to the* GOVERNOR)

A pitiful and miserable life.
I beg you, set this wretched fellow free.
2745　Whatever the offense he has committed,
His dreadful work is punishment enough.

(*To the woman*)

You shall have justice, woman. Make your plea
Inside the castle; this is not the place.

ARMGARD

No, no, I will not leave this spot until
The governor will set my husband free.   2750
He's been in prison for the past six months
And waits in vain to get the judge's verdict.

GESSLER

You want to force me, woman? Get away!

ARMGARD

I plead for justice, Governor! You sit
As judge in place of emperor and God,   2755
So do your duty here and give us justice
As you expect it for yourself from heaven.

GESSLER

Remove these shameless people from my sight!

ARMGARD (*seizing the reins of the horse*)

Oh no, you won't! I've nothing more to lose.
You will not leave this place, Lord Governor,   2760
Until you've granted justice. Roll your eyes,
Wrinkle your forehead, and scowl just as you please;
Our misery is so extreme that we
Don't fear your anger any more.

GESSLER

                                        Make room,

Unless you want my horse to step on you.   2765

Armgard

Then let it step on me.

> (*She pulls her children to the ground and throws herself down beside them in his way.*)

                              I'll lie right here
With my own children. There now—let your horse
Tread underfoot and kill these helpless orphans.
It will not be the worst thing that you've done.

Rudolf

2770   Are you completely mad?

Armgard (*continuing with greater vehemence*)

                              You've long been trampling
The kaiser's country underneath your feet.
I'm just a woman, but if I were a man,
I'd know a better thing to do than lie
Before you in the dust.

> (*The former music is heard again from the high point of the road, but more softly.*)

Gessler

                              Where are my men?
2775   Take her away before I lose my head
And do in anger something I'll regret.

Rudolf

Your men cannot get through just now, my lord.
The road's obstructed by a wedding party.

GESSLER

I'm still too mild a ruler for these people;
Their idle tongues remain too free. They still   2780
Are not completely tamed, as they should be.
But things are going to change, I give my word.
I'm going to break this stubborn mind of theirs;
This daring spirit of freedom I will crush.
I will proclaim a new and strict decree   2785
In all these lands. I will—

(*An arrow pierces him. He puts his hand on his heart
and is about to fall from his horse. His voice is feeble.*)

O God, have mercy.

RUDOLF

My lord! Oh God, what's this? Where did it come from?

ARMGARD (*getting up*)

It's murder, murder! He's falling down! He's hit!
The arrow struck the center of his heart.

RUDOLF (*jumping from his horse*)

What a dreadful thing! Oh God! My gracious lord,   2790
Cry out to God and pray to him for mercy.
You are a dying man.

GESSLER

That was Tell's shot.

(*He has slid from his horse into the arms of* RUDOLF
DER HARRAS, *who lays him down on the bench.*)

TELL (*appearing above on the cliff*)

You know the archer; you needn't search for others.
Our homes are free and innocence is safe.
2795 You'll do no further damage to our country.

(*He disappears from the cliff. People rush in.*)

STÜSSI (*running in ahead of the people*)

What is the matter? What has happened here?

ARMGARD

Someone has shot the viceroy with an arrow.

PEOPLE (*running in*)

Who has been shot?

(*While the first of the wedding party are coming on the stage, those in the rear are still on the height. The music continues.*)

RUDOLF DER HARRAS

                    He's going to bleed to death.
Get help somewhere! Pursue the murderer!
2800 Poor helpless man, so you must die like this.
You would not listen to my words of warning.

STÜSSI

Come look how pale and lifeless he is now.

MANY VOICES

Who did this thing?

RUDOLF DER HARRAS

    Are all these people crazy,
That they make music for a murder? Silence!

  (*The music breaks off suddenly. People continue to
  flock in.*)

My lord, speak if you can. Is there no message   2805
You would entrust to me?

  (GESSLER *makes signs with his hands, repeating them
  vehemently when they are not understood.*)

     Where should I go?
To Küssnacht? I can't understand. Don't be
Impatient, and don't think of earthly things;
Consider how to make your peace with heaven.

  (*All the people of the wedding party stand around
  the dying man in cold horror.*)

STÜSSI

Oh, look, how pale he is! Now death has struck   2810
His heart. His eyes are growing dim and closing.

  ARMGARD (*lifting up one of her children*)

Look, children! This is how a tyrant dies.

  RUDOLF DER HARRAS

You crazy women, haven't you any feeling,
That you can feast your eyes on such a horror?
Come help me! Lend a hand! Will no one help   2815
To pull the painful arrow from his breast?

WOMEN (*stepping back*)

What, touch the man whom God himself has struck?

RUDOLF DER HARRAS

Oh, curse you. Damn you!

(*He draws his sword.*)

STÜSSI (*seizing his arm*)

      Don't dare to do this, sir!
Your rule is past. The tyrant of our land
2820 Is dead. We will no longer tolerate
Your violence, for we are free men now.

ALL THE PEOPLE (*tumultuously*)

Our land is free!

RUDOLF DER HARRAS

     And has it come to this?
Obedience and fear so quickly ended?

(*To the soldiers and armed attendants who are pressing in*)

You men all see this monstrous act of murder
2825 Committed here. All help is now too late;
It does no good to hunt the murderer.
We're pressed by other worries. On to Küssnacht!
We'll try to save that fortress for the king.
For in this single moment are dissolved
2830 All bonds of order and obedience,
And we can trust in no man's loyalty.

(*While he is leaving with the soldiers, six members
of the order of the Brothers of Mercy enter.*)

ARMGARD

Make room, make room! Here come the Brothers of Mercy.

STÜSSI

The victim's dead, and so the ravens come.

BROTHERS OF MERCY (*form a semicircle around the
body and sing in solemn tones*) [11]

Death comes to us before our time
    And grants no respite from his power;   2835
He cuts us down in life's full prime
    And drags us off at any hour.
Prepared or not to go away,
    We have to face our judgment day.

    (*While they repeat the last two lines, the curtain
    falls.*)

---

[11] This song of the monks is meant to function like the chorus in
Greek tragedy. There is a musical setting by Beethoven, "Gesang der
Mönche" ("Song of the Monks").

ACT FIVE

Scene I

A public square at Altdorf.

(In the right background is the Uri fortress with the scaffold still standing, as in the third scene of Act One. To the left the view opens upon many mountains, on all of which signal fires are burning. It is daybreak, and bells are heard ringing at several distances.)

(Ruodi, Kuoni, Werni, the Head Mason and many other countrymen enter, accompanied by women and children.)

Ruodi

2840 You see the signal fires upon the mountains?

Head Mason

And do you hear the bells beyond the forest?

Ruodi

Our foes are driven out.

Head Mason

                  The castles are taken.

Ruodi

And we in Canton Uri still endure
The tyrant's fortress on our native soil?
2845 Are we the last to claim our liberty?

HEAD MASON

We let this yoke of bondage, meant for us,
Still stand? Let's tear it down!

ALL

                      Yes, tear it down!

RUODI

Where is the Ox of Uri? [1]

HORNBLOWER

                Here. What is it?

RUODI

Climb to the mountain watch, and blow your horn
So loud that it will sound from peak to peak   2850
And waken every echo in the gorges
To call together quickly all the men
From Uri's mountains.

    (HORNBLOWER *leaves.* WALTER FÜRST *enters.*)

WALTER FÜRST

               Wait, my good friends, wait!
We haven't heard from Schwyz and Unterwalden
What's happened there. Let's wait for messengers.   2855

---

[1] A literal translation of *Stier von Uri.* He is the official horn-blower and his horn is supposed to be made of the horn of the ure-ox (*Auerochs,* "aurochs, bison"). Tradition derives the name Uri from the old word "ure-ox," and the seal of the canton shows the head of an ox or bull.

RUODI

Why should we wait? The tyrant of the land
Is dead. The day of freedom has arrived.

HEAD MASON

Are not these flaming messengers enough,
That blaze on every mountain peak around?

RUODI

2860 Come, everybody, men and women! Come
And break the scaffold; tear the arches down!
Destroy the walls! Don't leave a stone in place!

HEAD MASON

Come on, you men! We built it, didn't we?
We know how to destroy it!

ALL

Tear it down!

(*They attack the building from all sides.*)

WALTER FÜRST

2865 It's under way. I cannot stop them now.

(*Enter* MELCHTAL *and* BAUMGARTEN.)

MELCHTAL

You let this fortress stand, when Sarnen lies
In ashes and the Rossberg has been stormed?

WALTER FÜRST

Oh, Melchtal, is it you? Do you bring freedom?
Are all the cantons rescued from the foe?

MELCHTAL (*embracing him*)

The land is free. Rejoice with me, my friend.   2870
Right at this very moment, while we're talking,
There's not a tyrant left in Switzerland.

WALTER FÜRST

How did you take the castles? Go on, tell us!

MELCHTAL

Young Rudenz boldly stormed the Sarnen castle
And conquered it in one courageous effort.   2875
I'd scaled the Rossberg's walls the night before.
But hear what happened. When we had driven out
The enemy and set the place on fire,
And crackling flames were leaping to the sky,
Then Diethelm, Gessler's page, dashed out and cried   2880
That Berta von Bruneck would be burned to death.

WALTER FÜRST

Oh gracious God!

(*The beams of the scaffold are heard falling.*)

MELCHTAL

                        She *was* in there. She'd been
Locked up in secrecy by Gessler's order.
Then Rudenz rushed in madly, for we heard

2885 The falling beams, the crash of heavy timbers,
And through the fire and smoke the lady crying
Piteously for help.

WALTER FÜRST

And was she saved?

MELCHTAL

That was the time for action and decision.
If he'd been nothing more than feudal lord
2890 To us, we would have thought of our lives first;
But he was our confederate, and Berta
Esteemed the people. So cheerfully we risked
Our lives for them and rushed into the fire.

WALTER FÜRST

But was she saved?

MELCHTAL

She was. Rudenz and I
2895 Together brought her from the fire and saved her,
While close behind the timbers cracked and crashed.
And when she realized she had been saved
And raised her eyes and saw the light of heaven,
The baron clasped me to his breast, and there
2900 A silent vow was sworn between us two,
A vow that will withstand the trials of fate
Because it's been annealed by glowing fire.

WALTER FÜRST

Where's Landenberg?

MELCHTAL

Across the Brünig pass.[2]
It's not my fault that he has kept his sight—
This man who had my father's eyes put out.   2905
I followed him and caught him as he fled,
And then I dragged him to my father's feet.
I had already drawn my sword above him,
But through the mercy of the blind old man
I spared his life as he lay pleading there.   2910
He swore a sacred oath he'd not return
And he will keep his word, for he has felt
Our might.

WALTER FÜRST

How good you've chosen not to stain
Our victory with blood.

CHILDREN (*running across the stage with fragments of
the scaffold*)

We're free! We're free!

(*The horn of Uri is blown with a mighty blast.*)

WALTER FÜRST

See what a celebration! These children will   2915
Recall this happy day when they are old.

(*Girls bring in the hat on a pole. The whole stage is
filling with people.*)

---

[2] On the southwest border of Unterwalden.

RUODI

Here is the hat to which we had to bow.

BAUMGARTEN

What do you think we ought to do with it?

WALTER FÜRST

Oh God! My grandson stood beneath this hat.

SEVERAL VOICES

2920   Destroy this emblem of the tyrant's power!
Let's burn it up!

WALTER FÜRST

No, let us keep the thing.
It used to be the sign of tyranny;
Now let it be the symbol of our freedom.

(*The countryfolk, men, women, and children, are standing and sitting on the beams of the wrecked scaffold,
grouped picturesquely in a large semicircle.*)

MELCHTAL

We stand here joyously upon the ruins
2925   Of tyranny, and what we swore at Rütli
Has come to pass today most gloriously.

WALTER FÜRST

The work has just begun, it isn't finished.
We need great courage now, and unity.
You can be sure the emperor won't wait

To avenge the death of his appointed ruler 2930
And reinstate the one we drove away.

MELCHTAL

Then let him come with all his mighty army!
Now that we have expelled the foe within,
We are prepared to meet the foe without.

RUODI

Not many passes lead into our land, 2935
And those we will defend with our own bodies.

BAUMGARTEN

We are united by a lasting bond,
And all his armies cannot make us fear.

(RÖSSELMANN *and* STAUFFACHER *enter.*)

RÖSSELMANN (*speaking as he enters*)

These are the dreadful judgments from above.

COUNTRYMEN

What is the matter?

RÖSSELMANN

What times we're living in! 2940

WALTER FÜRST

Speak up, what's wrong? Oh, Werner, is it you?
What is the matter?

COUNTRYMEN

What is it?

RÖSSELMANN

Astounding news.

STAUFFACHER

We're liberated from the gravest fear.

RÖSSELMANN

The emperor has been murdered.

WALTER FÜRST

Gracious God!

(*The countrymen are agitated and crowd around* STAUFFACHER.)

ALL

2945   Murdered? What? The emperor was murdered?

MELCHTAL

Impossible! Where did you get such news?

STAUFFACHER

It's true. King Albrecht was assassinated
Near Bruck. A truthful man, Johannes Müller,
Brought us the awful message from Schaffhausen.[3]

---

[3] Bruck is north from Zurich (not on the map), with the old Hapsburg castle not far away. Müller was a Swiss historian from Schaffhausen whose writings served as one of Schiller's sources.

WALTER FÜRST

Who dared to do so horrible a thing?   2950

STAUFFACHER

The man who did it makes the act more dreadful.
It was his nephew, son of his own brother,
Duke John of Swabia, who carried out the deed.

MELCHTAL

What drove him to this act of parricide?

STAUFFACHER

The emperor kept back the inheritance   2955
Of this impatient man. And it was said
He wanted to retain it for himself,
And then appease him with a bishopric.
However this may be, the duke inclined
His ear to bad advice from friends in arms,   2960
And with the noble lords von Eschenbach,
Von Tegerfeld, von Palm and von der Wart,
Decided, since he could not get his rights,
That he would take revenge, with his own hand.

WALTER FÜRST

Tell us, how did they do this dreadful thing?   2965

STAUFFACHER

The king was riding from his Baden castle,[4]
En route to Rheinfeld, where he held his court;
With him were Princes John and Leopold [5]

---

[4] Baden is in Canton Aargau, in northern Switzerland.
[5] Leopold was Emperor Albrecht's son.

And quite a train of noble gentlemen.
2970 And when they reached the landing at the Reuss,
Where you must get across the stream by ferry,
Assassins forced their way into the boat
And cut the kaiser off from his attendants.
Then as the king was riding onward through
2975 A cultivated field (where it is said
A city used to stand in pagan times),
Within clear sight of ancient Hapsburg castle,[6]
The birthplace of his royal lineage,
Duke John rushed at the king and plunged his dagger
2980 Into his throat, von Palm thrust with his spear,
And Eschenbach came in to split his skull.
And so he fell and lay in his own blood,
By his own kinsmen killed, on his own land.
Those on the other bank could see the crime
2985 But, separated by the stream, could give
No help, but only cries of futile anguish.
There by the wayside sat a poor old woman,
And in her arms the kaiser bled to death.

MELCHTAL

So he who took all things, but never gave,
2990 Has only dug his own untimely grave.

STAUFFACHER

A monstrous fear hangs over all the land.
The passes in the mountains are blockaded
And all the borders of the cantons guarded.
Old Zurich even closed her city gates,

---

[6] The *Habichtsburg* or "Hawk's Castle." The name developed into Habsburg or Hapsburg by elision.

Which stood unlocked and open thirty years,　　　2995
In fear of murderers, and worse—avengers.
For now stern Agnes, Queen of Hungary,[7]
Who has no trace of woman's tenderness,
Comes armored with the ban of outlawry
And would avenge her father's royal blood　　　3000
Upon the families of the murderers,
Upon their servants, children, children's children,
And even on the stones of all their castles.
She's sworn an awful oath to sacrifice
Whole generations on her father's grave　　　3005
And bathe in blood as in the dew of May.

MELCHTAL

You know which way the murderers have fled?

STAUFFACHER

They left right after they had done the deed
And took their flight in different directions,
So that they'll never meet on earth again.　　　3010
It's said Duke John is wandering in the mountains.

WALTER FÜRST

And so their crime will bear no fruit for them,
For vengeance bears no fruit. It is itself
Its own repulsive food, its sole delight
Is murder, and its satisfaction, dread.　　　3015

STAUFFACHER

Their crime will profit the assassins nothing,
But we will pluck with clean and unstained hands

---

[7] Albrecht's oldest daughter.

The blessed fruit their bloody deed produced,
For now we are released from greatest fear.
3020 The strongest foe of liberty has fallen,
And it's reported that the crown will pass
From Hapsburg's hands into another house.
The Empire will affirm its free election.[8]

WALTER FÜRST *and* SEVERAL OTHERS

Whom will they choose?

STAUFFACHER

                              The Count of Luxemburg
3025 Is favored most by the majority.

WALTER FÜRST

It's good that we were loyal to the Empire;
There's reason now to hope for right and justice.

STAUFFACHER

Yes, each new ruler needs to have brave friends,
And he will shield us from all Hapsburg vengeance.

(*The countrymen embrace each other. The* SACRIS-
TAN *and a* ROYAL COURIER *enter.*)

SACRISTAN

3030 Here are the honored leaders of our country.

RÖSSELMANN *and* SEVERAL OTHERS

What have you there?

---

[8] The German emperors of the Holy Roman Empire were chosen
by the electoral princes of the realm.

SACRISTAN

A courier brings this letter.

ALL (*to* WALTER FÜRST)

Quick, open it and read.

WALTER FÜRST (*reading*)

"To her good people
Of Uri, Schwyz, and Unterwalden, Queen
Elizabeth sends grace and all good wishes."

MANY VOICES

What does she want with us? Her reign is over.   3035

WALTER FÜRST (*reading*)

"In her great pain and widow's heavy sorrow,
In which the bloody passing of her lord
Has plunged the queen, she still bears in her mind
The ancient faith and love of Switzerland."

MELCHTAL

She never thought of us in her good fortune.   3040

RÖSSELMANN

Be still, let's hear the rest.

WALTER FÜRST (*reading*)

"And she expects of all these loyal people
That they will feel a deep and just abhorrence
Against the perpetrators of this crime.
Therefore, she now expects of all three cantons   3045

That they will give no aid to the assassins,
But rather that in fealty they will help her
Commit them to the hands of the avenger,
Remembering the love and former favors
3050 They have received from Rudolf's royal house."

(*The countrymen show indignation.*)

MANY VOICES

The love and favors!

STAUFFACHER

True, we received some favors from the father;
But what have we to boast of from the son?
Did he confirm the charter of our freedom
3055 Like all the other emperors before him?
Did he speak righteous verdicts or allow
Protection for mistreated innocence?
Did he so much as listen to the men
We sent to him as envoys in our anguish?
3060 Not one of all these things the king has done;
And if we had not by ourselves secured
Our rights by our own hands, courageously,
Our needs would not have touched him. Gratitude?
He sowed no gratitude within these valleys.
3065 He stood upon so high a place of power
He could have been a father to his people,
But he preferred to care just for his own.
Let those whom he has favored weep and moan.

WALTER FÜRST

Let's not rejoice about his fall. Let's not
3070 Remember now the wrongs that we endured.

May that be far from us. But that we should
Avenge his death, who never did us good,
And hunt down those who never did us harm,
Does not befit us, and surely can't be right.
For love must be a freewill offering,   3075
And death releases from enforced demands.
We owe him no more duties in these lands.

MELCHTAL

And though the queen is weeping in her chambers,
Lamenting in her wild despair to heaven,
You see a people here released from anguish,   3080
And giving thanks to that same heaven above.
Who would reap sympathy must first sow love.

(*Exit* COURIER.)

STAUFFACHER (*to the people*)

But where is Tell? Must he alone be absent,
The man who is the founder of our freedom?
He did the most, endured the hardest lot.   3085
Let's go as pilgrims to his house and call
Our praises out to him who saved us all!

(*All leave the stage.*)

SCENE II

The main room of TELL's *house.*

(*A fire is burning in the fireplace. The open door shows
the scene outside.*)

HEDWIG, WALTER, *and* WILHELM

HEDWIG

Your father's coming home today, my boys.
He is alive and free; we all are free.
3090 Your father is the one who saved our country.

WALTER

Now, Mother, don't forget I was there too.
They'll have to mention me. My father's arrow
Came very close, but I was not afraid
And didn't tremble.

HEDWIG (*embracing him*)

                    Yes, you're given back
3095 To me again. I've borne you twice, my son.
The pains of birth I've suffered twice for you.
But now it's past. I have you both again,
And your dear father is coming home today.

(*A* FRIAR *appears in the doorway.*)

WILHELM

Look, Mother, look, a friar's standing there.
3100 He must have come to ask us for a gift.

HEDWIG

Go bring him in, so that we can refresh him,
And let him feel this is a happy house.

(*She leaves, returning soon afterward with a cup.*)

WILHELM (*to the* FRIAR)

Come in, good man; my mother's bringing something.

WALTER

Come in and rest, and go away refreshed.

FRIAR (*glancing around fearfully with a wild, haggard look*)

Where am I? Tell me, what's the town and country?   3105

WALTER

You must have lost your way if you don't know.
You are in Bürglen, sir, in Canton Uri.
This is the entrance to the Schächen Valley.

FRIAR (*to* HEDWIG *as she enters*)

Are you alone, or is your husband here?

HEDWIG

I'm expecting him. But what is ailing you?   3110
You look as if you brought us nothing good.
Whoever you are, though, you're in need. Take this.

(*She offers him the cup.*)

FRIAR

However much I'm longing for refreshment,
I'll not take anything until you've promised—

HEDWIG

Don't touch my dress! Don't come too close to me.   3115

Stay farther back if you want me to listen.

FRIAR

Oh, by this hospitable fire, and by
Your children's precious heads I here embrace,
I beg of you—

(*He takes hold of the boys.*)

HEDWIG

                    What do you want? Get back
3120 And leave my boys alone! You're not a friar!
You're not! These robes are meant to harbor peace,
But there's no sign of peace in your expression.

FRIAR

I am the most unfortunate of men.

HEDWIG

Misfortune calls the heart to sympathy,
3125 But your appearance freezes all my feeling.

WALTER (*jumping up*)

Look, Mother, Father's here!

(*He rushes out.*)

HEDWIG

                    Heavens!

(*She starts to follow, trembles, and holds onto the
          door post.*)

WILHELM (*running after* WALTER)

It's Father!

WALTER (*outside*)

Now you are home again!

WILHELM (*outside*)

Father, Father!

TELL (*outside*)

Yes, I'm home again. But where's your mother?

(*They enter the house.*)

WALTER

She's standing by the door and can't get farther,
Because she's trembling so from fright and joy.   3130

TELL

Oh, Hedwig! Hedwig! Mother of my children!
Our God has helped. No tyrant parts us now.

HEDWIG (*clinging to him*)

Oh, Tell, Tell! I suffered anguish for you!

(*The* FRIAR *becomes attentive.*)

TELL

Forget it now, and live for joy alone.
I'm home with you again! This is my house,   3135
And I am standing in my place once more!

WILHELM

But Father, where's your crossbow? I don't see it.
Where is it?

TELL

You'll not see it again, my son.
I've had it put inside a holy place;
3140 It won't be used for hunting any more.

HEDWIG

Oh, Tell! Tell!

(*She steps back, letting go of his hand.*)

TELL

Why are you frightened, dear?

HEDWIG

But how have you come back to me? Oh God!
How do I dare to hold this hand? This hand—

TELL (*with warmth and spirit*)

Defended you and also saved our country.
3145 With conscience clear I raise it up to heaven.

(*The* FRIAR *starts up suddenly.* TELL *catches sight
of him.*)

Who is this friar?

HEDWIG

I had forgotten him.
You speak with him, I'm frightened in his presence.

FRIAR (*coming nearer*)

Are you the Tell who killed the governor?

TELL

I am. I don't intend to hide the fact.

FRIAR

So you are Tell. It must be Providence 3150
That's brought me here to you, beneath your roof.

TELL (*looking at him closely*)

You aren't a friar. Who are you then?

FRIAR

                   You killed
The governor who wronged you. I too have killed
An enemy who kept my rights from me.
He was your enemy as well as mine. 3155
I freed this country from its foe.

TELL (*starting back*)

               You are—
How dreadful! Children! Children, go in there.
Go with them, Hedwig. Go! You wretched man,
You must be—

HEDWIG

             Heavens, who is it?

TELL

             Don't ask.
Just go away. The children mustn't hear it. 3160

Go from the house. Go far. You mustn't stay
A moment here beneath this roof with him.

HEDWIG

Oh God! What is it? Come.

(She leaves with the children.)

TELL *(to the* FRIAR*)*

You are the duke
Of Austria. That's who you are! You've killed
3165 The emperor, your uncle and your lord.

JOHANNES PARRICIDA

He robbed me of my legacy.

TELL

You've killed
Your emperor, your uncle! And the earth
Still bears your weight? The sun still shines on you?

PARRICIDA

Tell, hear my side—

TELL

You're dripping with the blood
3170 Of murdering your kinsman and your kaiser.
How dare you step into my decent house?
How dare you show your face to honest men
And claim the right of hospitality?

PARRICIDA

I hoped to find compassion in your house.
You too have taken vengeance on your foe.   3175

TELL

You dare confuse ambition's bloody guilt
With a father's necessary self-defense?
Did you defend your children's heads from harm
And guard the sanctuary of the home,
Or shield your own against the greatest wrongs?   3180
I'll raise my guiltless hands to heaven above
And curse you and your deed, for I avenged
The laws of nature; you dishonored them.
I share no guilt with you. Your act was murder,
But I defended what's most dear to me.   3185

PARRICIDA

You cast me off, uncomforted, despairing?

TELL

I'm overcome with horror as we talk.
Away! Go on your dreadful road alone,
And let this house of innocence be pure.

PARRICIDA (*turning around, ready to leave*)

I cannot and I will not live like this.   3190

TELL

And yet I must have pity. God in heaven!
You're still so young, from such a noble house,
The grandson of my former kaiser Rudolf—

And now a fugitive assassin, pleading,
3195 Despairing, at my door—a poor man's door.
        (*He turns aside.*)

PARRICIDA

If you can weep, lament my awful fate.
It's horrible. I am a prince—or was one—
And surely could have lived in happiness
If I had curbed my own impatient wishes.
3200 But envy always gnawed my heart, because
I saw the youth of cousin Leopold
Endowed with honors and enriched with lands,
While I was kept like a dependent boy,
Although I was of equal age with him.

TELL

3205 Unlucky man, your uncle knew you well
When he withheld from you those lands and subjects.
You have yourself confirmed his wise decision
With your impulsive, shocking act of madness.
Where are your bold accomplices in crime?

PARRICIDA

3210 Wherever the avenging spirits drove them.
I haven't seen them since the woeful deed.

TELL

You know the ban of outlawry forbids
Your friends to help and gives your foes free hand.

PARRICIDA

That's why I must avoid all public roads

And do not dare to knock at any door.   3215
I turn my footsteps to the wilderness;
A terror to myself, I roam the mountains
And shudder at the sight of my own image
Whenever it's reflected in a brook.
If you have sympathy or human kindness—   3220

> (*He falls down before* TELL.)

TELL (*turning aside*)

Get up! Get up!

PARRICIDA

Not till you give your hand to me in help.

TELL

How can I help? Can any sinful man?
But stand up now. Whatever dreadful thing
You've done, you are a man, and so am I.   3225
No one shall go uncomforted from Tell.
I'll do for you what's in my power.

PARRICIDA (*jumping to his feet and grasping* TELL's
                hand vigorously)

                                                Oh, Tell,
You save my trembling soul from stark despair.

TELL

Let go my hand. You have to leave. You can't
Remain here undiscovered, and if discovered,   3230
You can't expect protection. Where will you go?
Where will you look for peace?

PARRICIDA

I do not know.

TELL

Then hear what God suggests to me. You have
To go to Rome, the city of St. Peter,
3235 And fall upon your knees before the pope,
Confess your guilt, and thus redeem your soul.

PARRICIDA

But won't he give me up to the avenger?

TELL

Whatever he does, accept it as from God.

PARRICIDA

How can I reach this unfamiliar land?
3240 I do not know the roads or where they lead,
And can't risk joining other travelers.

TELL

I will describe the road that you must follow.
You'll have to go upstream along the Reuss
That rushes wildly down the mountain gorges.

PARRICIDA (*frightened*)

3245 The Reuss? It was the witness of my crime.[9]

---

[9] Tell means the upper part of the Reuss that flows from the south
into Lake Lucerne. Parricida is referring to that part of the Reuss
that flows from the lake northward into the Aare and thence to the
Rhine.

TELL

The road leads you beside the gorge. Along
Its course are many crosses to remind you
Of travelers entombed by avalanches.

PARRICIDA

I'm not afraid of nature's threats and terrors
If I can tame the anguish in my heart.   3250

TELL

At every cross kneel down, and there confess
Your sins with fervent tears of penitence.
And when you've passed this road of horrors [10] safely,
And if the icy mountain doesn't send
An avalanche of snow to bury you,   3255
You'll reach the Devil's Bridge, which hangs in spray.
If it does not give way beneath your guilt,
Then when you've safely left the bridge behind,
A rocky gate will lead you to a tunnel—
As black as night, where daylight never reaches—   3260
And it will take you to a pleasant valley.
But you must hurry on with rapid steps;
You cannot stay where peace and joy abide.

PARRICIDA

Oh, Rudolf, noble ancestor, like this
Your grandson comes into your royal realm.   3265

TELL

Then, climbing still, you'll reach St. Gotthard's heights

---

[10] The road along the Reuss is called the *Schreckensstrasse.*

Where you will see the everlasting lakes
That draw their water from the streams of heaven.
There you will say farewell to German lands;
3270   From there another lively stream will lead you
Into your promised land of Italy.

> (*The Alpine cowherd's melody, sounded on alpen-
> horns, is heard.*)

I hear the people coming. You must leave.

HEDWIG (*rushing in*)

Where are you, Tell? My father's coming. And there's
A whole parade of fellow countrymen.

PARRICIDA (*hiding his face*)

3275   I cannot stay among these happy people.

TELL

Go, Hedwig, give this man some food and drink,
And give abundantly. His road is long
And he'll not find an inn along the way.
Hurry now. They're coming.

HEDWIG

                          Who is he?

TELL

                                            Don't ask.
3280   And when he leaves us turn away your eyes
So that you will not see the road he follows.

> (PARRICIDA *goes quickly toward* TELL, *but the latter
> motions him to stay back and leaves. When the two have*

left the stage in different directions, the scene changes,
showing the

Last Scene

The whole valley before Tell's *house and the heights that*
enclose it are crowded with countrymen who are grouped
in a picturesque tableau. Other countrymen are coming
along a high pathway and crossing a footbridge over the
Schächen.)

(Walter Fürst *with the two boys,* Melchtal, *and*
Stauffacher *come forward. Others crowd behind them.*
When Tell *appears, all greet him with shouts of joy.)*

All

Long live our Tell, deliverer and archer!

(While those in front are crowding around Tell *and*
embracing him, Rudenz *and* Berta *appear, the former*
embracing the countrymen, the latter embracing Hedwig.
The music from the mountain accompanies this wordless
scene. When it has stopped, Berta *walks to the center of*
the crowd of people.)

Berta

Confederates and countrymen, receive me
Into your union, the first so fortunate
To find protection in this land of freedom.   3285
I put my cause into your valiant hands.
Will you protect me as your citizen?

Countrymen

We will indeed, with life and property.

BERTA

Then I will give to this young man my hand,
3290 To live in liberty in this free land.

RUDENZ

And I declare my serfs and vassals free.

(*While the music begins to sound again, the curtain
falls.*)